FIELDWORK

Finding Home and Hope in Life's Changing Seasons

REBECCA COLLISON

ISBN: 978-1-967375-22-6 (Paperback)

ISBN: 978-1-967375-23-3 (E-book)

Library of Congress Control Number: 2025912307

Printed in the United States of America

Published by:

info@thequippyquill.com
(302) 295-2278

ACKNOWLEDGEMENTS

It takes many hands for a farm to yield something that brings life, and even more to make that farm a home. And I am thankful for those who have helped in the process that brought this published work to fruition. First and foremost, I thank God from whom all blessings and good gifts flow by His grace and for His glory. For without my Lord and Savior, home would not exist.

To my clergy colleagues and the churches I have served over the years, thanks for the challenge to go deeper and wider in exploring my theology from new perspectives. To my son Patrick and consultant Kim Brown at The Quippy Quill for encouragement to re-visit and give a fresh light to the first book I wrote, and your willingness to read and re-read my drafts.

I am forever grateful to my parents: my Dad, whose stories planted a love of reading and writing in me at an early age, and how he and Mom, along with Mimi and Pop, who nurtured my love of the Lord and my love of learning. I miss you all so much but your legacy lives on in me and many others.

To my sons - Randy, Robby, Patrick and Joe – it's been your willingness to transition from being a teacher's kid to a preacher's kid, and your grace through my "I have an idea moment" gave me the encouragement to put pen to paper. And to my entire expanded and extended family for your love and support no matter what crazy idea I get rambling about during family dinners.

And to Glenn, the man who has shown his support through the many days when papers and books had to be moved from the dining room table to make room for a late dinner, your love and encouragement made this work happen. While I apologize for not including all those who have encouraged me, believed in me, prayed for me, or simply said, "you go, girl", know that I thank you for giving of yourselves to make the garden of ideas grow into this book.

Rebecca "Becky" Kelly Collison

INTRODUCTION

My love for stories began at a young age. Growing up in the small town of Laurel, Delaware, stories could be found everywhere I went. From the country market where I bought penny candy to the farmers gathered at the local Southern States shooting the breeze to testimony time at our country church, stories surrounded me. But my favorite stories were the ones told by my father.

My father worked shift work at the area factory, so he wasn't always able to put me to bed. On those occasions when he was home at that time, he often read poems and stories to me; but the best nights were when he told me stories of his own creation. At times during my childhood, my grade school classmates and even the members of my elementary Sunday school class shared in my delight as my father spun a tale that was laid on his heart. The characters in his stories were fictional and yet they were familiar. My father's stories usually began with a person facing a challenge and, through interactions with other characters and situations, met the challenge by showing the strength of goodness and kindness. As I grew older, those stories ended and were replaced with true stories about people he met and incidents he encountered.

After high school, my endeavors continued to include the power of story as I worked as a small-town newspaper reporter for five years and then embarked on college, being the first member of my family to earn a bachelor's degree. Later, my career transition from special education teacher to United Methodist preacher saw my personal reclamation of the power of stories in life, but this time I was sharing the stories told in the Scriptures so others could connect the gospel of Jesus Christ to their everyday life. However, it took my entry into the Doctor of Ministry program at Wesley Theological Seminary to once again be reminded that story and spiritually healthy growth go hand in hand.

Having grown up within the agricultural-rich community of lower Delaware, I realized the land is where I found my true home. Not because I am a farmer or a gardener, because I do not have a green thumb. Yet time and time again, the farming landscape I took for granted was Jesus' most popular canvas for painting the gospel message of hope.

My doctoral project completed in 2019 involved some rural-based small churches in the local district of my denomination, with specific focus to my appointment to Wesley United Methodist Church, a small church within a rural town setting. My doctoral project titled. "Cultivating God's Farm: Using agricultural and biblical stories and seasons to reseed hope in small rural churches," was the result of two years of study and work with the faithful congregants of four area churches. Qualitative and quantitative data was shared in my first outing as an author in the book, "Preparing Fields in Seasons of Change". The book explained the learnings gleaned and offered a Bible study, an amended version of which is offered in this volume. Wesley UMC was my home for that season, a season of challenges and celebrations and lessons learned. And then the pandemic of 2020 changed life as I knew it.

Pastors at churches of all sizes learned how to adapt to a cell phone video on social media as their primary means of communicating the gospel of Jesus Christ. I still chuckle when someone says, "oh, I saw you on TV" when referring to an average Sunday morning service. On site services took on a new feel as shouted hallelujahs were replaced with honking horns of the attendees' vehicles in the church parking lot, with pastors standing on flatbed trailers or even pickup truck beds to shout out the Good News. And that was not the only change in this season.

It was during 2020 that the word "disaffiliation" grew louder as the denomination of which I had cut my theological teeth was preparing for a major shift. During the years that followed the pandemic shutdown, the denomination I had called home was breaking apart. And by 2022, I left the church home base I knew and went a familiar but new direction. Wesleyan theology and Methodist traditions still shaped my faith, but from a different structure.

As "Preparing Fields for Seasons of Change" was originally written to help small rural churches within a changing landscape, I realized its lessons helped me navigate through the many seasons of change that I would face in the following years. It was during this time that "Groundwork: Farm Parables and the Cultivation of Faith" was written to help draw others, including myself, back to the Scriptures for guidance and direction. The season I had just encountered rocked my world: changes that made me question who I was and where I belonged. Leaving me with the question, "Where was home when home had changed?"

In 2025, as the dust settled, I took my original manuscript of "Preparing Fields" and revisited the lessons that were applicable in every season of change. By changing the title to "Fieldwork," a new focus emerged. With the Old Testament book of Ruth as an underpinning, and upon the advice of two people from different segments of my life, I wrote this book. Ruth's story is one of the heart as the field where life grows and where changes are experienced in life, changes that can make or break one's faith. The story of Ruth's journey of letting God work the field of her life for His good is a story that echoes commonalities among all of the children born of the land in the Garden.

See, each generation has narratives that hold hopes, fears, history, and faith of people across the ages. Each person has a story, and each church has a story. And the best stories were the ones told when we were at a place where we were open to receive. The stories are heard in testimonies, in song, over a cup of coffee with a neighbor, and even in the midst of tears while sharing concerns in prayer time. Especially in the rural community where I grew up and have lived most of my life, relationships were made and strengthened by shared stories. The farmland found in abundance in the southern part of Delaware also told a story of seasons that are beyond human control but provide the necessary framework for the growth of fruit in the land. Our life narratives bear witness to who God is and who we are, for our stories are markers of where we have been and where we are going.

The doctoral project, begun almost 10 years earlier, opened my heart and mind, not only to my own story but to my connection with others as they shared their stories. Within the community, we see the image of God, and it is through the stories of our experience; we can see the fullness of God. For the land is not just a pile of dirt for one thing to be grown, it is a stage for the divine diversity and holy creativity spoken of in Scripture to be made tangible. And sacred diversity is what was shaping my reclamation of and understanding of how one's true home shape's identity more than just a place or person.

The birthing place of new expressions of faith emerge from Jesus' call to love God and love neighbor from the life fields of heart, soul, mind, and strength (ref. Mathh. 21:37-39, Mark 12:30-31). From the field of our heart, emotions, affections, and desires are born to express our love for God, not only in worship and praise, but in how we care and share that love with others. From the field of our soul, comes our spiritual nature that is the very eternal breath that blows across our very being as we engage others in authentic community. Our minds are fields in which our intellect, understanding, and reasoning take root as we seek knowledge to make informed decisions based on God's wisdom in our everyday lives. Additionally, our physical bodies are meant not only to embody the holy but also to be a resource of energy, abilities, and possessions in service to God and to edify others we meet and serve in our daily walk of life. In essence, all of these fields must be employed to bring about wholeness in a holistic fashion, where every part of our being is a dedicated landscape to offer life in relevant and genuine ways to others with whom we share life on this earth. God's farm includes the four key fields of one's life in order to grow up a faith that feeds those hungry for truth, justice, and compassion. The fruit of the four fields of God's farm in our lives is only possible when we cultivate the fields in and out of season, as shown in the Old Testament book of Ruth.

For that reason, I have included former lessons learned from those small rural churches and my own life, placing them alongside the heart fields found in the story of Ruth.

Chapter one establishes the understanding of land from a scriptural and agrarian point of view. Scriptural and scholarly references underpin the relevance of land-based seasons. Correlations with spiritual seasons are offered along with the introduction of soul soil.

Chapter two opens the pages of the Old Testament book of Ruth that begins in the fallow season. While loss seems to permeate the opening chapter, under the surface is a compilation of spiritual nutrients that will give life in the appropriate time and place. This chapter also encourages the reader to be still and listen to the land of their heart to know who they are, even if in foreign territory.

Chapter three offers a view of Ruth in the planting season of her life from Ruth 2 of her biblical story. Seeds of humility and kindness combine to bring life into what seems to be a barren field. As roots begin to grow deep in her new faith, Ruth sees the emergence of hope in unexpected places. Being faithful in this season also offers hope to others around her, for none of us lives in a vacuum.

Chapter four explores the growth of the seeds of faith planted in Ruth's life, seeds that result in growing relationships and the emergence of trust. This growing season shows the change from her being seen as a foreigner to being a woman stepping out in confidence. While weeds and challenges crop up in the growing season, this is where the fields of the heart grow in identity and promise. One's roots go deeper into the soil of the soul during the growing season. A discussion of spiritual pollinators is also shared.

Chapter five offers a look at the harvest season as the efforts of Ruth's spiritual farming have come to fruition, which feeds not only her spirit, but the lives of others. The harvest season also looks at the diverse ways the landscape of our lives and our community are impacted by the efforts of others. Ruth's legacy, much like our own, does not just occur from her faith, but from the seeds of faith in her heart that spread into generations to come, bringing salvation to all.

Chapter six asks the question, "what's in the field of your heart?" and offers the reader a land-based approach their current season and situation. Scripture points the individual to the opportunity and diversity that not only builds up the Body of Christ, but also a vibrant witness difficult to contain. At the back of the book, two six-week studies are offered: a study constructed for personal faith growth and devotional study and a separate study created for use in a small group for faith and discipleship development.

The land is a part of our lives in ways often forgotten or minimized, for as my grandfather, Pop, often said, "Don't forget where you come from – that's the stuff you are made of." And the making of identity is an ongoing shaping and molding process by the seasons of life. Seasons change so that we can be changed; instead of fighting or bemoaning the change, we can prepare the fields of our heart to receive the new transformation offered. The land where we find ourselves – whether dirt fields or paved streets, wooden barns or steel skyscrapers - speaks to our wandering soul who searches for home, whether in familiar or foreign landscapes around us. So let us return to the land from where we have come to reclaim the life that is forever rooted in the echo of The Garden of the Creator. So, come hear the story afresh and let it change the rich soul soil in the field of your heart.

CONTENTS

Chapter 1

SEASONS CHANGE

My kids call my husband Glenn vanilla, because he likes things how he likes things. Predictable. Familiar. Nothing too "out of the box." (And this makes me smile, because God made him a pastor spouse – talk about living into the unpredictable. However, if he can control a situation like the lights on the house at Christmas or the seasoning added to the roast chicken, he adapts to little changes. In short, change is acceptable if he still feels comfortable. And that can be said of most people. How many of you have a favorite place to sit at an event, a preferred way you like your coffee, or where the thermostat should be set?

Growing up on the farm, he always anticipated the change in the agricultural seasons: a time to plow, a time to plant, a time to harvest and store, a time to rest, and then a time to repeat it all over again. However, storms came into those seasons. Heat waves created new challenges. And when the harvest was lower than anticipated, the waiting season of fallow fields seemed to take longer than expected. Yet, the familiarity of cold winters and warm summers was welcome because the identity of the land was consistent. If the season was a bad one, it would pass. And if the season was a good one, it also would pass in time. A farm was willing to be consistently transformed by the season that came without permission or request.

Witness Lee spoke to the understanding of God's Farm – the life found and offered in the relationship between Creator God and two interconnected creations: the land and humankind. He said, *"A farm is a plot of land for growing things. The church is God's land to grow Christ, not in an individual way, but in a corporate way...something of Christ will be grown up in each of us."[1]*

Since the beginning, land has been a central theme in biblical faith and a key component in understanding one's relationship to God. Agrarian references throughout the Bible are not just a reflection of the economic and societal landscape from ancient times, but a template for one's individual spiritual growth in discipleship and for the growth of the church. Through the lens of the land, the human story of faith unfolds and informs the missional call of every believer – to grow in order to bear fruit.

The role of the land and its relevance to the lives of God's people can initially be seen throughout the Hebrew Bible. As author James Weldon Johnson referenced Genesis 2:7 in poetic verse:

Up from the bed of river, God scooped the clay;

And by the bank of the river, He kneeled him down;

And there the great God Almighty

...kneeled down in the dust

Toiling over a lump of clay

Till he shaped it in his own image;

Then into it he blew the breath of life,

And man became a living soul.[2]

Dietrich Bonhoeffer writes "humankind is derived from a piece of earth and its bond with the earth belongs to its essential being".[3] Bonhoeffer continues that "human beings have their existence as existence on earth".[4] From this agrarian viewpoint, the land-humankind connection goes deeper than just God's creation of humankind's form out of dust. Ellen Davis, an agrarian theologian, explains the land-humankind connection in more detail.

> ... agrarians know the land, not as an inert object, but as a fellow creature that can justly expect something from us whose lives depend on it..."And YHWH God formed the human being ['adam], dust from the fertile soil ['adama] (Gen. 2:7) Although the wordplay is captured surprisingly well by the English pun "human from humus", the Hebrew is more fully descriptive of the family resemblance. Thus 'adam from 'adama is localized language; it evokes the specific relationship between a people and a particular place.[5]

From creation in the Garden of Eden, to Noah's finding a place to land after the flood (Genesis 8), to Abraham's leaving his land of origin (Genesis 12), to Joshua setting foot upon the Promised Land (Joshua 1-5), humankind, namely God's people, have been connected to God through the land. The land-referenced as desert, orchard, fields, vineyards, mountains, and more – was seen as geography and political property. The covenantal gift for Abraham, the inheritance of the Promised Land, meant stability and a place of physical belonging for God's people.

Theologian Walter Bruggeman notes that the "Hebrew term 'eres functions to refer both to earth and land; in its usage as earth, the term clearly refers to the created earth with reference to the creator God who governs heaven and earth.[6] He continues that the same term, however, refers to land, most specifically Israel's "land of promise" that Israel hopes for and holds from Yahweh. Bruggeman's assertion is that the land is for all heirs of the covenant, even those who have no power to claim it.[7] According to Bruggeman, the land for all is the single central symbol for the promise of the gospel.[8]

The Old Testament book of Ruth is a beautiful offering of how God not only prepares fields of our lives for what is to come, but also plants seeds of faith through events and people. The book is told through the actions of three main characters: Naomi the widow, Ruth the Moabite which marks her as a foreigner, and Boaz the Israelite. As the story unfolds, the intersection of their lives takes place in foreign and familiar landscapes, as home is redefined for each over the course of the four chapters. The unfolding of how their lives touch future generations is also seen in the New Testament as Ruth's role in the genealogy of the Coming Messiah is included in the Gospel of Matthew, Chapter One.

In the New Testament, the understanding of whom the land is for and what the land means to God's faithful takes on a new depth of significance. Jesus and his apostles developed a new understanding of the Land, which saw the earlier focus on a physical land as a necessary means of preparing for God's purpose to "bless all nations" through Abraham's seed -   the blessings of being "in the land" were now available universally through Israel's Messiah "in Christ".[9]

Jesus Christ brought the understanding of the life-giving land and its expanded role in spiritual growth and discipleship to his teachings in the New Testament. Jesus, who was born in a farm structure (Luke 2:7), taught with agrarian based parables to help connect people of faith with the land to which they were inextricably connected by creation and by livelihood.   These parables include: Grain on Sabbath, Matt. 12:1-8; Sower, Matt. 13:1-9, 18-33; Mustard Seed, Matt. 13:31-32; Weeds in the Wheat, Matt. 13:24-39; Worker in the vineyard, Matt. 20:1-16; Tenants in the Vineyard, Matt. 21:33-46; Budding Fig Tree, Matt. 26:32-35; Rich Man and Bigger Barns, Luke 12:15-21; Barren Fig Tree, Luke

13:6-9; and the Prodigal Son, Luke 15:11-24. Other agrarian references throughout the Gospels include the importance of the vine (John 15) and the role of the laborers for the Kingdom of God. (Matt. 9:27, Luke 10:2)

For the land, and the people of the land, to serve God, faith would be required, and that faith would develop in cycles, much like the seasons of the agricultural landscape. Ecclesiastes 3 reminds one that "for everything, there is a season", and that as long as earth endures, the land will undergo seasons. (Gen. 8:22)

In the Bible, the word season or time emerges as two separate words in the Greek language: Chronos and Kairos. Time is measured by the date on the calendar, but also by the moments and experiences in our lives. In short, Chronos is about minutes, Kairos is about moments. Both ways of measuring time are important, and both are controlled by Creator God, but it is the Kairos that has more significance in reclaiming our spiritual vitality. For while Chronos measures time, Kairos measures the value of a faith experienced.

Even corners of society who do not know the difference between a corn field and soybean field understand the concept of seasons. Look at the shelves of the local stories and you will see the seasons according to the marketing professionals who stretch a particular time of year to make the most sales. And yet the land offers a more organic and true view of a season. The land's agricultural seasons mirror the seasons of faith experienced by people of God throughout the Old and New Testaments patterned in four basic stages: *fallow, planting, growing* and *harvest* seasons. While each season may look different within different geographic areas, certain elements remain constant. Similar seasons are experienced in the spiritual lives of those created from the land; that is, all humankind and specifically God's people. By examining each season and its connection to the spiritual self, one can begin to see the correlation between the physical land and the spiritual life.

First, the *fallow season* is characterized by weather conditions and landscape that are not conducive to widespread planting in the outdoors, and empty fields are found. The time of not planting and not growing can be seen as a time of Sabbath for the ground. In Genesis, God rested on the seventh day. And in the Ten Commandments, God instructs us to do the same: "Remember the Sabbath day, to keep it holy. Six days you shall labor, and do all your work, but the seventh day is a Sabbath to the LORD your God." (Exodus 20:8) While even Psalm 23:2 suggests a Sabbath for the people, the land also must have a Sabbath, a time when planting and growing are not seen.

> But the seventh year you shall let it rest and lie fallow, so that the poor of your people may eat; and what they leave the wild animals may eat. You shall do the same with your vineyard and with your olive orchard.
>
> Six days you shall do your work, but on the seventh day you shall rest, so that your ox and your donkey may have relief, and your home-born slave and the resident alien may be refreshed. (Exodus 23:11-12 NRSV)

Hymn writer Natalie Sleeth, who was in a season of feeling loss and grief following a friend's death,[10] remembered the line from a T.S. Elliot poem: "In my beginning is my end"[11]. Sleeth wrote the "Hymn of Promise" which helps us understand the unseen power and hope of the fallow season:

In the bulb there is a flower; in the seed, an apple tree;

In cocoons, a hidden promise: butterflies will soon be free!

In the cold and snow of winter there's a spring that waits to be,

Unrevealed until its season, something God alone can see.[12]

The bare empty field of uncertainty is also seen in scripture passages such as Jeremiah 32, when God instructs Jeremiah to buy land in a season that does not seem to be fruitful or promising to the human eye. However, the fallow season of the land and the fallow season of the spirit are necessary in the life of God's people.

Theologian Howard Thurman writes:

> There is a fallow time for the spirit when the soil is barren because of sheer exhaustion... whatever may be the seasons, one has to deal with the fact. Face it! Then resolutely dig our dead roots, clear the ground, but don't forget to make a humus pit against the time when some young or feeble plants will need stimulation from past flowering in your garden. ...the time is not wasted. The time of fallowness is a time of rest and restoration, of filling up and replenishing. It is the moment when the meaning of all things can be searched out, tracked down, and made to yield the secret of living. Thank God for the fallow time.[13]

In the agricultural and spiritual timeline, the fallow season is followed by a planting season. The planting season of the land is defined by favorable weather and landscape, which show readiness to be turned over and plowed in order to receive seeds and new plantings. In the Old Testament, the prophet Hosea shows the connection between the planting season of the land and the planting season of the soul by referencing a time to "sow for yourselves righteousness; reap steadfast love; break up your fallow ground; for it is time to seek the LORD that he may come and rain righteousness upon you." (Hosea 10:12 NRSV)

Planting season is highlighted by the turning over of the ground to create new growth. In spiritual growth required in discipleship, to create or construct a new understanding, one must first destroy the current status quo from a new perspective, turn over the land for a fresh receptivity, and decide which seeds to plant based on the value of the relationship with God and others. Jesus, as the Master Gardener, cultivates the spiritual landscape in order to bring about new life. (John 12:23-24) The planting season is most clearly illustrated in Scripture by the Parable of the Sower, which tells of seed that is broadcast and the state of the soil upon which it falls, determining the fate of the seed in both the physical and spiritual lives of God's people. (Mark 4:3-9, 13-20; Matt. 13:1-9, 18-33). The planting season involves breaking up the hard ground to allow for gospel seeds to take root, removal of rocks that inhibit growth in challenging situations, and looking out for the thorns that choke out any fruit-bearing potential.

From the planting season, the land and the spiritual pilgrim must embark upon the *growing season*, a season characterized by the land which has received the seed, and whereupon maturation from seed to plant takes place. Jesus' agrarian parables continue to address the growing season specifically with celebrations and challenges that accompany the physical growth on the land and the spiritual growth of the believer.

Celebration in the *growing season* is seen in the Parable of the Mustard Seed (Matt. 13:31-32), where the seed of little faith grows exponentially and benefits more than just the farmer. Challenges in the growing season are also apparent, as they are seen in the Parable of the Weeds in the Wheat (Matt. 13:24-39) and the

Parable of the Barren Fig Tree (Luke 13:6-9) where the farmer in charge of monitoring the growth of the plant has to trust God's timing and God's plan, and not rely on one's own understanding of the growing process. These *growing season* parables inform individual believers and the church of what is required in order to bring about fruit for the Kingdom.

The Apostle Paul also explains the dynamic between humans as the farmer and God the Creator.

> I planted, Apollos watered, but God [all the while] was causing the growth. So, neither is the one who plants nor the one who waters anything, but [only] God who causes the growth. He who plants and he who waters are one [in importance and esteem, working toward the same purpose]; but each will receive his own reward according to his own labor. For we are God's fellow workers [His servants working together]; you are God's cultivated field [His garden, His vineyard], God's building. (1 Corinthians 3:6-9, Amplified Bible)

In summation of the *growing season*, God does the growing, but God's people have to be good stewards of the land given and the opportunities availed.

The fourth season of the land is identified as *Harvest;* a time when the growing period of a particular crop is completed and the crop is taken out of the field to be dispersed in various ways. In the Old Testament, the harvest is described as a time of blessing for the one who planted (Deut. 24:19) and the one who didn't plant (Lev. 19:9). Specifically, the story of all of the seasons, and especially the significance of the harvest, can be seen in the Old Testament book of Ruth, a story that depicts the process from fallowness, to the planting of hope, to the growing of that hope, to the harvest of grain and of blessings to future generations. In the Ruth 2 passage, where Ruth is gleaning the fields, protection and provision are offered at the harvest as not only the lineage is protected, but generations to come will be provided by the fulfillment of the promised Messiah. But the harvest is not just about bringing in crops for the present age; the spiritual harvest is dependent upon the state of our heart, as seen in Jesus' parable about the Rich Man and the Bigger Barns. As God stands in control of the harvest (Jere. 5:24, Amos 4:7), so Jesus is the Lord of the harvest of God's Kingdom (Matt. 9:38).

The Apostle Paul's writing in 1 Corinthians spells out the importance of the land in God's purpose for believers:

> Do not be deceived; God is not mocked, for you reap whatever you sow.[8] If you sow to your own flesh, you will reap corruption from the flesh; but if you sow to the Spirit, you will reap eternal life from the Spirit.[9] So let us not grow weary in doing what is right, for we will reap at harvest time, if we do not give up.[10] So then, whenever we have an opportunity, let us work for the good of all, and especially for those of the family of faith. (Galatians 6:7-10 NRSV)

As land is created by God, humankind is created of the land and given life by God, and is thereby connected to the land both physically and spiritually; in short, we are God's farm for a purpose – a reality that has been seen through the ages.

Chapter 2

PREPARING TO COME HOME

When he came to his senses… he headed home to his Father
(ref. Luke 15:17,20)

Home. Over the years, I have called many places home: a rented farmhouse, a single-wide mobile home, a second-floor apartment, the spare room in someone else's house, a house built on the corner of the family farm. By other definitions, home was the place where my parents lived, where my grandparents lived, where I raised my own sons. And yet those definitions fall flat because home is more than places or people: people and places can and do pass away.

Seasons of life transform us on purpose for a purpose. Leaving the place where you were raised from childhood. Having to move to a different city or country due to work. Changing how you live due to the birth or death of a loved one in your life. And at times, finding change you never asked for and didn't want to begin with. Seasons in life shape our identity as our understanding of home is transformed.

When the Apostle Paul talked about the body of Christ, he encouraged a deeper meaning of home, when he reminded the church, "We are God's workers, working together; you are like God's farm, God's house." (ref. 1 Cor. 3:9). A church home may be where you attend for your entire lifetime or only a season, depending on the reality of your life. Yet, wherever you call home, a farm is being formed in the soil of your soil. Transformation is happening to make life–new life – happen. Finding the landscape where one can thrive has always been embedded deep within people of all nations and cultures.

Theologian M. Craig Barnes notes that we all have a longing for home that can be traced back to the Garden, a paradise that will never be realized as such on earth. However, home is not just a place we like; it is our longing to get to the place where life seems right again.

"(Home) it's the right place, the place where we belong, where we know who we are, who we are, and are no longer bothered by the revealing light…at home, life feels just so right. That's because it is a place where the saved communion has been restored and made right."[14]

Through the years and across continents, the farming frontiers have been a canvas upon which Jesus, as the agrarian theologian, made his point with broad strokes. Specifically, through the formative years of the American landscape, the relevance of the agricultural landscape upon the faith is acutely understood by the people who claim small rural churches as their home and identity. The small rural church played a significant role in the circuit rider tradition in the early years of the Methodist movement. As the circuit rider would go from town to town in the early days of America's expansion, so the message of the Gospel would be seeded, planted, nurtured, and grown. One specific method of growth could be found in the camp meetings. Frederick Norwood writes: Camp meetings were the few occasions when people were gathered together in large numbers…Camp meeting time came "between the wheat harvest and the time for gathering corn".[15]

Research from 2020 reveals 70% of all American churches are considered small churches.[16] Small churches of less than 100 people in Sunday worship have faced their own challenges as they sought to grow within the changing landscape. Holding on to one's spiritual grounding as the literal ground beneath their feet has changed in the past century has proved especially challenging for rural churches. Even though the theological significance of the land has not changed, how society views the relevance of faith in the 21st century has shed a new emerging need for spiritual renewal and grounding in society. What constitutes a spiritual home must not be based on sentimentality, but on spiritual vibrancy.

Scholar Walter Bruggeman addressed the dilemma of changing sociopolitical and economic dimensions, noting that Biblical faith and the God of the Bible cannot be left disconnected from real public life in the world.[17] Bruggeman continues that "Loss of place and yearning for place are dominant images in contemporary culture".[18] He claims that a sense of space is a primary category of faith: specifically, place is space that has historical meanings where some things have happened that are now remembered and that provide continuity and identity across generations.[19]

For Bruggeman, humanness, as biblical faith promises it, will be found in belonging to and referring to that locus in which the peculiar historicity of a community has been expressed and to which recourse is made for purposes of orientation, assurance, and empowerment.[20]

> Human connectedness to the land is suggested in biblical language by a play on words. '*Adam*, that (is, humankind, has a partner and made, '*adamah* (land) … a sound theology requires honoring covenantal relationship. The operating land ethic in our society denies that relationship at enormous cost, not only to land but to our common humanity.[21]

While society yearns for a home, social media posts give evidence that society is living in such a way that has disconnected many from the life-giving land, making them spiritually homeless. Much like dirt. Dirt is actually displaced, homeless soil. Soil is the compilation of minerals, air, water, animals, and other living matter that accumulates in layers and becomes compacted over time. When particles of the soil erode or are dug up, they lose the "history" of their place, their grounding of home. One scholar noted that soil is a diverse but integrated community of living and inanimate things that make up the ground beneath our feet. The soul of each person on God's farm has either soul soil rich for growing or dirt that has become disconnected.

The disconnection from the spiritual grounding of the land, once known through the small church, has been directly affected by the farm crisis and rural focus decline in recent years. Author Kathleen Norris addresses this issue based on her experience with the rural communities in the Midwest. In her book, *Dakota: A Spiritual Geography*, she notes that "while not minimalizing the sufferings inflicted on the Native Americans, the farm crisis of the 1980s leads her to believe that farmers are the next Indians... losing one's land and facing massive national indifference. . . .one (person) asked the question, 'how many of us are going to stand beside the farmer and see justice done for these people?'."[22] She continues by sharing glimpses of hope, as seen through a small rural church called Hope that depicts the resiliency of the land with the resiliency of grounded faith in the rural-based faith community. She notes that the song "Nearer My God to Thee", is a rural hymn that the city people don't fully understand, but those who live close to the land embrace fully. She writes:

> I wonder if a church like Hope doesn't teach the world in the way a monastery does, not by loudly voicing its views but existing quietly in its own place...I wonder if what Columba Stewart, a

contemporary Benedictine, has said about such earthy metaphors, that "the significance of field, vineyard and garden metaphors in biblical post-biblical texts... lies beyond their relevance to the agricultural economy of ancient peoples."[23]

Norris continues that Hope's church members take seriously their responsibility as members of the world's diverse and largely poor human race.[24] As an example, she cites that while Hope's membership declined by nearly half in recent years, the amount the church donates for mission has increased every year.[25]

Truth is, our lives are set between dynamics of losing and expecting, of being uprooted and re-rooted, of being dislocated because of impertinence and being relocated in trust.[26] To maintain our grounding, we need to return to our identity as those who Creator God formed from the earth and infused with God's own Spirit. Theologian Jürgen Moltmann explains this grounding as humans seeing themselves as the product of nature and theologically as imago mundi.[27]

Human being as 'a creature in the fellowship of creation...' before we interpret this as being as *imago Dei*, we shall see him as imago mundi – a being that can only exist in community with all other created beings and which can only understand itself in that community.[28]

Diana Butler Bass, in her book, "*Grounded: Finding God in the World – A Spiritual Revolution*", expands on the idea of our identity being spiritually founded with the earthen ground: God is the ground, the grounding, that which grounds us. We experience this when we understand that soil is holy, water gives life, the sky opens the imagination, our roots matter, home is a divine place, and our lives are linked with our neighbors' and with those around the globe. This world, not heaven, is the sacred stage of our times.[29]

Diana Butler Bass explains in reference to Mark 4:8 that Jesus' seed is God's love, and the soil is us, so the moral of the story is that we are not "soily" enough.[30] She writes: God is a dirt farmer, not a vegetable gardener. Soil is not sin. Soil is sacred, holy, and good. When we care for it, we are doing God's work. Soil is life. And it is time for us to reclaim the dirt.[31] Davis expands on how humankind can reclaim the dirt through the biblical story. She supports the theory that "the things the biblical writers must themselves have intended as important conveyors of meaning, become intelligible when the Bible is read from an agrarian perspective

Davis continues that the Israelites of the Scriptures survived as farmers by becoming intimate with the land, by learning to meet its expectations and its needs, and by passing on their knowledge, with each generation serving as the human "seed stock" indispensable for the well-being of the next.[32] The passing of this information was accomplished through the spirituality involved within the act of storytelling.

Home is where identity is found because it is where stories are birthed into being. Stories told and stories lived through a particular season shape and transform our understanding of life and faith. In the story of Ruth, Naomi leaves her home because of a famine. Ruth leaves her home due to marriage into another family. Both women then must once again leave the home created together to journey and start anew without their husbands. Boaz does not journey from the family farmlands he owns, but his journey is one of giving his heart to point to the prophetic love that redeems.

The search for spirituality "brings down to earth, plants the feet firmly on the ground, and allows a vision of self as it is, as we are imperfect and ambiguous."[33] In this search for spirituality, the story emerges from true speaking and true thinking to create a connection between the land from which humans were formed and the Spirit which brings the form to life.[34]

Theologian Howard Thurman understood the sacred connection whereby life comes from our innate grounding with the earth and our Creator. He wrote: "God is the source of the vitality, the life, of all living things. His energy is available to plants, to animals, and to our own bodies if the conditions are met. Life is a responsible activity. What is true for our bodies is also true for mind and spirit." [35]

Life happens because the biblical stories are combined with the stories of the land for a holy connection. Those who live on the land are in tune with the power of community, not just for accomplishing the task at hand, in and out of season, but also for continuing the sacred stories which grow and feed one's faith in the One who is Love. The relationship between the land and its seasons and faith in God, with its spiritual seasons, provides a grounding that the small rural church is uniquely designed to offer.

Author Daniel Stulac writes about his experience at a little country church, located in a rural community historically devoted to animal husbandry, which decides to hang a portrait of Christ the Good Shepherd in the front foyer of the chapel. He wrote that this faithful congregation chose to characterize its faith through a portrait of Christ the farmer...

> Christ, whose arms are wrapped around a sheep. Christ, who knows late nights in the barn and early mornings in the pasture. Christ, who knows the backbreaking work of hay season. Christ, who

knows the gut-wrenching worry of a failed harvest...Christ of the compost pile. Christ of the filthy fingernails. ... The gospel of Jesus Christ is a gospel of emplacement. It is good news born in a barn. It is a gospel of the ground.[36]

He continues that "We are, quite literally, born of dust. But that does not mean we are only dust. Filled with the breath of God, we have a special vocation, too – to serve the garden in which God placed us, and to keep it well. We are creatures designed by God to have our hands dirty; we are intended for cultivation."[37]

Cultivation is a process by which soil is broken and turned over to allow for new growth. The biblical and agrarian stories within the walls of the small rural churches found in agricultural landscapes can help us once again claim our identity as people whose spiritual grounding comes from the dirt to which we return. For the God who formed humankind in Eden, on purpose, is still cultivating our spirits in the farmlands where rural churches call home and where the stories remind us that we are all part of God's farm.

In the creation of the land, we experience a groundedness in the identity we share with the Creator of the land. Any study of the land through a theological lens means that one must distinguish a church with a "soil" culture and a church with a "dirt" culture, specifically in the realm of small rural churches where not all were alike in their level of health and vitality. A "soil" culture church recognizes the diverse and integrated community that is layered in history and defined by place: the *soil* church is alive and offers to share that life. A "dirt" culture church does not have the integrated layers of community and history and has no place to call home; the *dirt* church exists but is not life-giving and is essentially suffering from spiritual homelessness. In other words, soil lives while dirt exists.

Likewise, for any person seeking their true purpose and spiritual home base, one must look to the land through the words of Scripture and the stories around them.

With the soil-dirt definition, a process of linking the local church's story, the biblical narrative, and the agrarian discourse was necessary for re-discovering their true spiritual home and calling. But to know the land, one needs to be in touch with the land. In the case of small rural churches used during the doctoral study, I used a LAND approach to address the current situation of a church I pastored called Wesley to determine the next faithful steps of bearing fruit on God's Farm in any season. The following chapters will address each letter in the acronym LAND, and additional resources are provided at the back of this book.

Yet maybe you are not in a small rural church. Maybe you are trying to find a spiritual home in the city. Maybe you are trying to find the current status of the soil in your soul. Maybe you have forgotten what home looks or feels like. If so, this journey is also for you. So, let's go to the land and reclaim our true home.

Chapter 3

L – LISTENING TO AND LEARNING FROM THE LAY OF THE LAND

*First this: God created the Heavens and Earth—all you see, all you
don't see… God looked over everything he had made; it was so good,
so very good!*

(Genesis 1:1,31 MSG)

It is not uncommon to find a farmer walking the property, row by
row, from day to evening. Not only does the farmer do this to find
the section of fencing where the cows got out or to see the blight
on the beans up close, but also to look and listen to the land. The
land has stories to tell, but one has to walk it, come in physical
contact with it, and be in relationship with it in all seasons in order
to learn from it. Listening to the land is not just an activity for when
life feels good or when one wants something from the land. When
one listens, one can hear the stories the land tells and the stories
it doesn't tell. The same is said of each of us: we long to be known
and long to be heard. Both corporately and individually, the
identification of our current season and the spiritual lay of the land
in our hearts must happen before we can even think about where
our identity-shaping roots need to go deeper. In other words,
where do we go where everyone knows our name and is glad that
we came?

The 21st century has made its mark on the small rural church
and its role in society. Small town, agricultural-based communities
saw an exodus of people to areas that offered more opportunities
in the social and technological culture of the times, and with the
exodus, some small churches found fewer people in the pews.
Mega churches with digital screens, online live streaming and

podcasts gave church goers more options than the single service at the small rural church. However, blending into the landscape of a larger crowd can occur if smaller group connections are not created and nurtured. Feeling lost in the crowd is another common side effect of the "bigger is better" approach.

The 2020 pandemic exacerbated the divide and sense of loss. The lack of on-site churches gave way to preachers now appearing on screens and social media to share their message. Instead of handshakes as they departed, many would give a thumbs-up icon from their smartphones. The change in how the church was conducted also changed how the community was created. And in the forefront of technological advances, disconnection from one's spiritual grounding increased. Scriptural holiness no longer led to social holiness; many "stopped meeting together" for prayer and study and went straight to serving others. Faith without works is dead, but works with no faith is like a person with no place to call home. While a purpose was served, the church building was becoming quickly a land with no nutrients for growing spiritual fruit. And without the seed-laden fruit, the people perish.

L.H. Bailey once wrote "into this secular and more or less technical education we are now to introduce the element of moral obligation that the man may understand his peculiar contribution and responsibility to society; but this result cannot be attained until the farmer and every one of us recognize the holiness of the earth."[38]

To address the issues related to the uncertainty of the seasons of rural agriculture, one must know the lay of the land and be familiar with its past as well as its present condition. Similarly, the rural church is in an uncertain season of existence yet has resources within its past seasons and the current "lay of the land" of its faith.

In the rural churches, the agricultural seasons of *fallow time, planting, growing,* and *harvest* find their resonance in the church calendar. Homecoming services are usually held at harvest time, when the corn, hay, and soybean crops are ready to be brought in. Fallow or wintertime, when the fields are bare, is when most of the farming community takes time off, and church Bible studies are usually better attended. Planting season in the spring usually sees local farmers working longer days, often strategically planning to avoid spring rains. The growing season is a time of monitoring the plants but also offers time for gathering at the state fair or other events before the harvest season comes again.

The resonance of the seasons is not only seen in church, but in our individual lives and in one's lived out faith. Follow seasons when all seems to be bare, like Naomi and Ruth at the loss of their husbands, which puts their foreseeable future in question. The book of Ruth opens with the fallow season in full swing in Ruth 1:1-5:

> In the days when the judges ruled, there was famine in the land. So a man from Bethlehem in Judah, together with his wife and two sons, went to live for a while in the country of Moab.[2] The man's name was Elimelek, his wife's name was Naomi, and the names of his two sons were Mahlon and Kilion. They were Ephrathites from Bethlehem, Judah. And they went to Moab and lived there.
>
> Now Elimelek, Naomi's husband, died, and she was left with her two sons. They married Moabite women, one named Orpah and the other Ruth. After they had lived there about ten years, both Mahlon and Kilion also died, and Naomi was left without her two sons and her husband.

While the book begins with fallow fields, moving to a new home physically, spiritually, and emotionally opens the pair of widows to a new future. A planting season where new roots are put into the landscape of their lives, placed with hope in an unseen promise. A growing season that emerges through the grit and grace of working through challenges, circumstances, and unseen dangers. And a harvest season where all things can visibly be seen coming together for the "good of those who love the Lord."

Closeness to the physical land can draw one closer to the biblical significance found in agrarian scriptural references. Favorite songs include "In the Garden", "Trust and Obey", and "Great is Thy Faithfulness", while favored scriptures in the rural church tend to come from Genesis, Ruth, and from Jesus' agrarian parables. However, society demands that "bigger is better" and that "technology reigns" are sentiments that have separated some rural churches from their grounding and inherent rootedness to the land. Masanobu Fukuoka, a farmer theologian, noted that "To the extent that people separate themselves from nature, they spin out further and further from the center."[39] He added that "farming used to be sacred work... Farming, as an occupation, this is within nature, lies close to this source".[40] To be connected with one's source is to be connected with one's identity.

Knowing the identity, or lay of the land, in a church can uncover untapped resources and begin the work and dealing with the challenges.[41] Goleman suggests "good storytelling can honor what they accomplished in the past, cull the wisdom that was there, and help reframe new practices for the future".[42] Mann notes that specific geographic setting is key to a congregation's story, since congregations are born from a generative spark of interaction between stories of faith and stories of place.[43] Mann continues that place-based narratives provide "here" with a trajectory that stretches over time, including remembered past, present reality, and an outline of imagined futures.[44]

In Berlin and Weems' book, "High Yield", leaders are reminded that ignoring the culture can be the downfall of wonderful visions for a newly imagined future. The authors relate the story of how a relatively new pastor was shown that culture matters to growth, as the new pastor proposed a specific community outreach program.

> The response was always the same: "We're just farmers. We can't do what other churches do." This culture was new to the pastor... he started viewing the vision of outreach through the lens of their culture. Soon, he realized that providing food for a range of people without sufficient food was a need in the community. A vision emerged around "food for the hungry." Sure enough, those who seemed instinctively to resist new ideas spoke up: "Pastor, we can't do that. We're just farmers." Immediately, the irony was evident to them and others. "Of course, we can do that. That's who we are. That's what we do. We are farmers. We feed the world.[45]

To learn the lay of the land in one's life, one must look and listen. The first thing to look at is to know what season you are currently in before hitching your identity to a group that does not recognize your current reality. For example, is the church or group you are looking to connect with a dirt church without life-giving layers or a soil church that has multiple rich layers?

When my son moved to another state, he looked for a church to join. While not an experienced "church shopper", he wanted a place where he could feel the Spirit of God moving, where the Scripture was taught, and where real-life situations were acknowledged as part of God's work in progress. In other words, he wanted the place he went to listen and learn from him as much as he was willing to listen and learn from them. No matter the culture, ability level, gender, socioeconomic situation, or social status, our identity is transformed and shaped when we open ourselves to what God is offering in the place where we land.

In the Bible, Abraham, Joseph, and even Paul would not have chosen some of the situations in which they found themselves; yet in each season, they listened and learned as the Spirit led them. By the shaping of their faith, they went on to teach others about the inclusive and diverse love of God for all humanity. As Jesus says in John 3:17, "God did not send his Son into the world to condemn it, but to save it." Jesus listened first to understand the lay of the land in a person's heart.

Too often, when engaging in conversation with someone new, we tend to hear them but not listen. Hear the words being spoken, but simultaneously determining in our minds how we are going to respond. Active listening and truly being present help, one learns the lay of the land for someone else. Employing the eyes of veteran saints and of newcomers for each offers a different perspective to be offered for a more complete picture. However, I found the stories to be the most telling of the current lay of the land. To focus these stories from a spiritual perspective, I employed a method called story linking used by Anne Streaty Wimberly in her book, "Soul Stories".

The strength of the story-linking process is seen when the agricultural narrative is connected to the faith stories of small and rural-based churches. Stories shared from beauty salons to bean fields may vary in focus from the climate affecting the field to the climate affecting the legislative assemblies, but all help form the identity of a people. While some stories are painful and others are buried under a protective veneer, the leadership of the church had been struggling with ways to bring forth their story and hear God's voice anew. The story-linking process with the culturally specific agrarian-based narrative allowed the reclamation of what is sacred, organic, and real; in essence, the process promoted their connection to each other, to God, and to the land in an increasingly technological world that seems to have forgotten its roots.

Saint Paul had said that we – God's people, the church – are God's farm (ref. 1 Cor. 3:9 NCV), so the same principles of reclaiming farmland in God's name could help reclaim the spiritual vibrancy that identifies God's people called to bear fruit. Author Noah Sanders notes four basic principles of the biblical worldview of agriculture:

We don't own our farm (Gen. 1:26).

Farming is not about us (Luke 12:15-21);

God knows more about farming than we do (Rom. 1:20); and

We can't make things grow (1 Cor. 3:7).[46]

The same agricultural principals apply in today's culture: if we want our churches – even small groups - to produce the fruit that God desires, then they need to acknowledge the basic principles related to the church as God's Farm (1 Cor. 3:9 NCV) and be rooted in the soil of the Word of God. If we, as members of God's farm, want to thrive in our spiritual identity, we must follow the same principles. We must come home to the land by knowing the lay of the land where God has placed us. In other words, pay attention so we can bloom where we are planted.

As a child going off to school for the first day, my parents made sure I knew my address and phone number, in case I got lost or missed the bus. As I grew older and began driving without a GPS, I found markers that pointed me in the right direction: the white house on the corner, the country store at the crossroads, the big willow tree in the yard. Using the familiar landmark method was abruptly dismissed when, in a new town, a helpful soul told me I could find the location I needed by walking across the street from where the Dollar General burned down five years ago. Needless to say, since I had only been in town five days, that person's landmark moment was not going to be very helpful for me. Spiritually speaking, one can not depend on the spiritual markers in someone else's life to identify where their spiritual grounding is found.

Masanobu Fukuoka, in *The One Straw Revolution*, wrote, The ultimate goal of farming is not the growing of crops but the cultivation and perfection of human beings.[47] The connection of soil and spirit is expanded by Wendell Berry: The soil is the great connector of lives, the source and destination of all. It is the healer and restorer and resurrector, by which disease passes into health, age into youth, death into life. Without proper care for it we have no community because without proper care for it, we have no life.[48] In other words, we become spiritually homeless.

To know the layout of the land, one must physically be in contact with the land and experience its past and its present to acknowledge where one truly is in their journey. Only then can the spiritual farmer move forward in planning and ploughing for new fruit to be brought forth. Only then can we come to our senses and return to our roots.

Chapter 4

A – ASSESSMENT AND ACKNOWLEDGEMENT OF THE GROUND ITS IDENTITY

He taught them many things by parables, and in his teaching said: "Listen! A farmer went out to sow his seed…

(Mark 4:2-3 NIV)

Any farmer knows that not everything grows well everywhere. Rice likes to grow in a wet environment because the abundant water keeps the weeds at bay, but wheat needs a drier landscape. Just as any true assessment of the one-size approaches at the department store clothing rack will tell you, people are not all one size either. Any season can offer comfort or discomfort. Any season can offer encouragement or discouragement. Every season offers new knowledge about ourselves and how we love God and neighbor as part of the fruit-growing process. However, one has to be honest in self-reflection.

In the opening verses of Ruth, the writer tells how a family of a husband, wife, and two sons left their homeland of Bethlehem – which ironically means bread – and traveled to the foreign country of Moab. While there, the husband dies, and the two sons marry local girls from this pagan culture. Then the sons die, and the women are left to fend for themselves in a patriarchal culture. When the widow Naomi hears that the famine has ended, she wants to go back to her homeland. In doing so, she releases the two foreign women who have married into her family, encouraging them to go back to their respective homes now that they are no longer bound in marriage. One leaves, but one named Ruth is determined to stay. By staying, Ruth acknowledges her choice will result not only in a change of location, but also a change in identity. Ruth 1: 15-18 shows this acknowledgement of the current life landscape and the choices to be made.

> "Look," Naomi said to her, "our sister-in-law has gone back to her people and to her gods. You should do the same."

> But Ruth replied, "Don't ask me to leave you and turn back. Wherever you go, I will go wherever you live, and I will live. Your people will be my people, and your God will be my God. Wherever you die, I will die, and there will I be buried. May the LORD punish me severely if I allow anything but death to separate us! "When Naomi saw that Ruth was determined to go with her, she said nothing more."

Not only will Ruth be seen as having a Moabite origin, but she is willing to be redefined by the next chapter in her life will be seen with the move.

Naomi, the widow, is filled with bitterness at the loss of family and groundedness she has faced in recent years and yet is willing to let the younger widow Ruth accompany her to the new chapter that will change both of their lives. Ruth's determination and Naomi's pain acknowledge the unknowns in their season of loss.

Addressing the appropriate season then lends to acknowledging that season. By definition, the verb "to acknowledge" means to accept or admit the existence or truth of a situation. One example of acknowledgment may be noting a dirt landscape as having rocky areas where one may need to spend extra time removing obstacles; it does no good to start planting spiritual seeds if the land is not ready to let those roots go deep. Likewise, one should acknowledge the dry areas that need more "living water" saturation through healing and assurance, the poor soil areas that need rich nutrients found in a vibrant spiritual relationship with Christ, and the hard soil that needs to be humbly and gently broken so it can be turned over and make room for new life to occur.

As was mentioned in the growing season, there are challenges that emerge to stop the change from seed to rooted plant to full-fledged crop; one cannot stop because of the challenges, but take them in stride as the wheat and weeds grow up together with grace. One needs to recognize the celebrations and the challenges of being faithful in the season you are in, instead of wanting to be somewhere else. Once a person is in a relationship with and learning from the land, and addresses the current situation accordingly, then comes the third step.

The rear-view mirror on a car was made smaller than the windshield for a specific reason: it was never meant to be the destination of the driver. Honest assessment of where one has been is a must, but once that is done, one's view must be forward. Jesus made this same observation when a would-be follower had a list of conditions before submitting to His Lordship: "Jesus replied, "No one who puts a hand to the plow and looks back is fit for service in the kingdom of God." Luke 9:62.

The Apostle Paul echoes the same sentiment from the farming perspective, "Brothers, I do not consider myself yet to have taken hold of it. But one thing I do: Forgetting what is behind and straining toward what is ahead, I press on toward the goal to win the prize of God's heavenly calling in Christ Jesus." Phil. 3:14-15. Any farmer will tell you that looking opposite from the direction of your goal will land you in a ditch, in the woods, or worse. Not to mention rows that are askew and witness to a walk that is all over the place. Focus on the land that is right in front of you to find your way.

Throughout my life, when I needed to clear my head, walking those fields – whether freshly plowed, expectant with seed embedded beyond my sight, or knee high with soybean plants, there was a peace, a connectedness with God, that I would take for granted and not reclaim until I was much older and wiser. As a pastor now back in the agricultural landscape that helped create me, I found a small rural church that I loved struggled with the season in which it found itself. So, I shared the pecan tree story told by theologian Howard Thurman:

> I watched him for a long time. He was so busily engaged in his task that he did not notice my approach until he heard my voice… He was an old man – as I discovered before our conversation was over, a full eighty-one years. Further talk between us revealed that he was planting a small grove of pecan trees. The little treelets were not more than two and a half or three feet in height. My curiosity was unbounded.
>
> "Why did you not select larger trees to increase the possibility of your living to see them bear at least one cut of nuts?
>
> Finally, he said, "These small trees are cheaper, and I have very little money."
>
> "So, you do not expect to live to see the tree reach sufficient maturity to bear fruit?
>
> "No, but is that important? All my life, I have eaten fruit from trees that I did not plant. Why should I not plant trees to bear fruit for those who may enjoy them long after I am gone? Besides, the man who plants because he will reap the harvest has no faith in life.[49]

Thurman concludes that all of life is planting and harvesting. No man gathers merely the crop that he has planted; this is another dimension of the brotherhood of man.[50] Thurman's story is a reminder that growth and health can never be dependent upon one person or one planting in one place.

While the saints have been faithful in their generation, the following generations reaped the harvest but forgot to replant with the intention that the yield is not specifically for them in their time. One particular church's past approach was seen in limited risk-taking, internal focus, and fundraisers for the church to meet its bills. Few mission-related endeavors were attempted in those years, and of the ones that were, risk was minimal. Financial focus obscured some of the necessary faith-development focus needed to sustain and grow a healthy and spiritually vibrant church.

In short, opportunities were missed because their view was not only in the rear-view mirror, but also at their own feet. A view of God's kingdom that does not go past our footprint will not reveal the divine identity in any of us. And even so, God persists in running to the prodigal, willing to return and will do more than we can hope or imagine accomplishing on our own. Hope and faith are priorities for the farmer tending the land; hope and faith should also be priorities for you and me, no matter the landscape where we currently reside.

With the source of the culture and economy being rooted in the surrounding land, the source of the spirituality of God's people could also be rooted in that same land but from a slightly different perspective. Place-based narratives are resources to consider that emerge in the rich stories from one's own backyard, a backyard created specifically by God for "such a time as this." Narratives help identify what has been and can help create a future narrative built on hope and faith

If the Bible and the land reflect the seasons of our lives, would the combination of stories and seasons also give direction for cultivating spirituality to bring hope and health into the one's current situation? To answer this question, I had to take on a farmer's mentality and process.

In my years of growing up in southern Delaware, I observed that farmers have different roles in different seasons. In the winter when the fields are fallow, farmers took the time to get equipment ready for the upcoming season; this was also the time for farmers to rest and reflect while letting nature take the rested land and breathe new life into it. The fields looked empty and bare, and yet the farmer knew that there was transformation occurring under the surface.

In the spring, the equipment was used to prepare the ground by cultivating it or turning it over to plant seeds. Seed was chosen for a specific need and tailored to the environment where it could thrive. Fertilizer and other nutrients were applied to help the seed die to self and grow into the plant it was destined to become.

Summer saw the growth of crops, often accompanied by the presence of new challenges. During the growing season, farmers protected their crops from damage by weeding and treating for insects. Invariably, some crops were lost, but many continued to grow due to the constant attention on bringing the crop to its full potential. While the farmer didn't make the plants grow, it was the farmer's responsibility to be diligent and proactive.

When fall came with its cooler temperatures, harvest was the focus of the farmer. The entire farming community seemed to be fully involved in the hard work of getting the crop from the field to the table in a timely manner. Timing was essential because of the uncertainty of the weather, which could destroy the yield. While the seed died to itself when planted in the ground months before, the fully realized plant was called to die to itself once again at the harvest. However, each time it died, a new opportunity for future growth was generated.

Much like a farmer who does not put all of his eggs in one basket, I could not seek healthy growth in only one area of the church. Farmers I knew had a main crop like feed corn, but also had one section of the farm for a smaller, secondary crop like watermelons, and an area for the hogs or cows. The diversification used in farming is used as a safeguard if disease or low prices put the farm in financial difficulty; it also allows the farm to offer more than just one thing.

Before starting to plant any seeds, silence and solitude are needed to hear God's plan, rather than simply relying on one's agenda or method. Taking the Scripture verse, "Be still and know that I am God" (Psalm 46:10) to heart, the practice of prayer was reintroduced as a manner of hearing from the land and its Creator God. If one never interacts with the land, understanding of how to "be still and know God" will not just emerge. Two-way communication through prayer builds a fertile relationship with the Lord for roots to go deep.

The spiritual discipline of prayer is essential in the life of a spiritual farmer. By saturating the ground with the rich spiritual nutrient of prayer, guidance can be received on when and where to go and do, or not do. Being faithful in the current season must occur before future plantings are attempted. Every season has its celebrations and challenges; therefore, any season a church finds itself in has potential for growth if one follows the markers.

Many people familiar with the look of a plowed field were amazed at how straight the lines of planted seed are arranged. The straight lines of most fields were made possible by ridge markers that mark where the center of the tractor should drive (while planting) on the next pass after the one the farmer is currently on. In this manner, each row would be lined up perfectly parallel to the one just before it. The farmer went through a methodical process of taking each row at a time, one by one, and side by side. Taking the cue from the farmer's planting process, the small church realigns itself to its mission, one row at a time, aligning itself over and over again with the marker that sets the standard.

Since prayer is the standard set in Scripture over and over again, it became the marker with which the church set out to ready the field for the seed the varied stories would bring. From Old Testament saints like the psalmist David, Hannah, and Daniel to Jesus' words on prayer from the Mount and the cross (Matt. 6:5-15, Matt. 7:7, Luke 23, John 19) to the Apostle Paul's exhortations to the early church (1 Thess. 5:16-18, Phil. 4:6-7), prayer is more than a wish list of what we want, prayer opens the heavens to an intimate loving relationship with an infinite powerful God. The experience of each person praying results in a story that magnifies trust and hope in the most difficult of circumstances. And we all have a story to tell. The question is, "Does the story hold life-giving seed for another person?"

To effectively use personal experience stories in finding one's spiritual identity, the story must be rooted in truth beyond opinion or assumption. Linking stories we tell with the places and people we know, and the God we want to know more, offers a beginning to our journey of reclaiming our true home.

The story linking process was originated by Anne E. Streaty Wimberly within her study, found in "Soul Stories: African American Christian Education". She explains:

> Story–linking is a process whereby we connect parts of our everyday stories with the Christian faith story in the Bible and the lives of exemplars of the

Christian faith outside the Bible. In this process, we link the Bible stories by using them as mirrors through which we reflect ... by linking with Christian faith heritage stories, we may be encouraged and inspirited by predecessors who have faced the circumstances with which we readily identify. The story-linking process can help us open ourselves to God's call..."[51]

Wimberly's focus was to "bring forth liberating wisdom and hope-building vocation" by linking the everyday story with the biblical story, then adding the culturally specific story of African American faith heritage to elicit a response of concrete action that would reveal a way to authentically live in the image of Jesus Christ.

An adaptation of Wimberly's process uses the linking of the everyday story with the Biblical narrative, but then, after linking those two stories, views them through an agrarian-based narrative, with the final link being made with a concrete action bridging the congregation and community. Basically, story linking is the process of connecting a personal story with a Bible story and then looking at it through the lens of the landscape or community where one finds themselves.

By replacing Wimberly's focus on the culturally specific story of African American faith heritage with the culturally specific focus of the agricultural narrative, the stories would more readily resonate with those in small rural or country churches. Stories rooted in the land where the people lived, worked, and worshipped permeate the community and would create a cohesive thread to connect with the land and its Creator God.

To begin this type of approach, an overview of the story-linking process was necessary. Wimberly's approach focused on four components in the story-linking process, with the first being engagement of the everyday story. She began with the understanding that every person has a story that defines who they are and how they got here, a narrative that has been influenced by other narratives gleaned from social contexts, life events, and interpersonal relationships – all the pieces that form one's identity.

While Ruth and Naomi's stories become intertwined, they become their own small group community. No person is meant to go through life alone. No field ever has only one seed. We only truly find ourselves, and even our true home, when we are in an authentic community.

The dynamic of the small group community provides fertile ground for stories to be told. As Sensing writes, we all have stories existing and being created in each socio-historical context; accordingly, our future stories are continuously written and constructed through dialogical human interaction and a dialogue of multiple voices. Narratives foster listening to the multiple voices emanating from ever-emerging and developing contexts. When people let you hear their stories, they are sharing a sacred trust, for it is through their stories that they give meaning and interpret their lives.[52] For that reason, I took each season and showed them how to link their stories with the four seasons of the land and the spiritual seasons as seen in the Bible.

The first session of the research study focused on the first of the four seasons to be addressed: the *fallow* season. From an agrarian perspective, the fallow season is when fields are bare and nothing seems to be growing. For many in the Mid-Atlantic region, this season is experienced as winter. Using the image of a fallow field, the following descriptors come to mind: sad, cold, bare, anxious, wanting, dormant, time of rest, and a time of reflection. Some people note the fallow season as their least favorite season, but others find it a much-needed season due to the ability to rest from one's work on the farm. Fallow seasons point to loss, and yet loss must be experienced in order to gain.

The Biblical story found in Jeremiah 12:1-25 and Exodus 23:11-12 helps unpack the idea of the power of the fallow season. In a small group discussion I once led, the question was asked, "Where is God in the *fallow* season as seen in the everyday story and the biblical narratives?" In response, many responded that the fallow season may not seem to have a positive aspect, but it is in the fallow season that the ground is renewed to ready itself for the next planting. It was also noted that the following season provided downtime and Sabbath to wait on God and strengthen trust in God. One person wrote:

> Snow is a distinctive feature of the winter season. While the ground is fallow, the snow is nature's own fertilizer. As the snow melts, it not only waters the ground but any farmer knows it infuses nitrogen into the ground naturally, thus making the soil richer for when the planting season comes around. It may not be our way or our time, but God's way and God's time are always best.

At this point, the agricultural narrative, the culturally specific story in the story linking process, was shared and further linking was made in relation to the fallow season. One woman I spoke with in that small group shared that the fallow season gives us a change to restore and regenerate because the consequence is that we can burn out and not be productive if we don't slow down so we have to step back to be able to step forward and let God be God.

The second session of the research study addressed the *planting* season. The image of artist Vincent van Gogh's 1888 painting called "The Sower" was presented on the opening page for the planting season and was used as part of a Visio Divina reflection and prayer. From an agricultural perspective, the *planting* season is when ground is turned over to make room for a new planting and plans are put into motion to fertilize and nurture the new growth. In the planting season, a farmer must often cultivate – pull up and turn over – the soil by reshaping it so it can accept the seed and water needed to grow. For many in the Mid-Atlantic region, this season is experienced as Spring. Using the image of a *planting* season field, participants were asked to give physical, emotional, and spiritual descriptors of the season. All groups shared descriptors such as being busy, seeing plowed rows and hearing tractors, anticipation of warmer weather, weather starts to change, being intentional, fresh earthy smell, rejuvenation, new life, desire to get out and go. One person in the small group study noted that when the dirt was turned over, it looked different because it went from dry brown to moist black with the promise of growth to come. Another participant noted that it's amazing how everything grows once the soil is turned over, but it also sometimes gets stinky in the process.

As the second session focused on the *planting* season progressed, the story-linking process brought in the biblical text from Jesus' parable of the sower in Mark 4:3-9, 13-20 and John 12:24. Once again, smaller breakout groups or pairs were created where the participants read the scripture and discussed what was going on in the story, who was in the story and how the descriptors for the *fallow* season could be seen in the story. Within this dialogue, links between the descriptors, the everyday story, and the biblical story were being made. As the group gathered back together to share, the question was asked, "Where is God in the planting season as seen in the everyday story and the biblical narratives?"

From the Parable of the Sower, a discussion of the soils was applied to the challenges in the planting season in the agricultural setting and in the local church setting. All agreed that the John scripture was a reminder that just as a seed needs to die to be born into a new life, we too need to die to ourselves spiritually and the process of planting requires either time, energy, or effort be given up from all of us. One participant noted that "life has ups and downs and my life is a field constantly getting turned over, so I have to trust God, have faith, and seek him before I make my plans". The participant went on to share that sorghum – a type of grain similar to corn – grows in quantity but is not as profitable because the nature of the crop "gums up" everything so it takes a lot more to make it profitable; in like fashion, we need to be prayerful of what we plant and why because the need may be present but may require more of us than we are willing to give.

In sharing the agricultural-based narrative, which shares challenges of the *planting* season, the theme that resonated was that we must be intentional, flexible, and patient as we do what we can and leave it with God. The songs "Great is Thy Faithfulness" and "Trust and Obey" are songs that resonate with whether we are doing new things, or other things in a new way, we must pray for God's guidance first and continue to plant seeds to God's glory. One participant shared the following reflection:

> When my boys were little, there was a corn plant that grew next to the mailbox. We didn't know how it got there. But there it stood all by itself. The mailman commented on it. The neighbors commented on it. One day, my little boy, Scotty, said, "It's mine, Momma." "I put it there. I planted it near the mailbox." So, we made a sign that said, "Scotty's corn," and, don't you know, that one stalk even grew ears of corn. Goes to show that if you plant a seed, it doesn't matter where growth can happen.

The message that emerged from all the groups was that in the *planting* season we need to be intentional and go forth and plant, and not just hope something grows. While growth is not always seen on the surface, and seasonal bugs of doubt and frustration can emerge, the spiritual farmer will at least always try.

The third session of the study addressed the *growing* season. The image of a farmer overlooking a field of growing crops was used to help initiate conversation. From an agricultural perspective, the growing season is defined as a time when conditions are favorable for growth; a time when fruit begins to emerge, and a time when challenges are encountered but perseverance prevails. In the Mid-Atlantic region, this season is usually known as Summer.

Descriptors used by the participants for the *growing* season included: excitement, green, beauty, fresh start, transitions, hope, worn, tentative, the need for attention and care, and challenges of wind, rain, frost, weeds, and pests to the emerging plants. For the local church, the growing season manifests in different ways.

One man in the study also made this observation:

> Every five years, apple orchards are cut down. New trees are planted to bring about the best fruit. Then it takes a few more years to see the yield of fruit. But the interesting thing is that you need more than one apple tree for the pollination process to work. The fruit depends on pollination; it's not a solo endeavor. The same can be said of the church; it's never been a solo endeavor.

As the third session focused on the *growing* season progressed, the story-linking process brought in the scriptural references of Matthew 13: 24-20 parable of the Wheat and the Weeds, Matthew 13:31-32 parable of the Mustard Seed, and Luke

13:6-9 parable of the fig tree that didn't yield. The 1 Corinthians 3:6-9 passage regarding Paul, Apollos, and God's role in growth was also included. In smaller breakout groups or pairs, the participants read the scripture and discussed what was going on in the story, the characters in the story, and how the descriptors for the *growing* season could be seen in the story. Within this dialogue, links between the descriptors, the everyday story, and the biblical story were being made. From the biblical stories, the participants gleaned the following insight:

- We love all and let Jesus do the weeding, or we could damage the good.
- The mustard seed plant not only grew bigger than expected but also served others in a way that wasn't planned.
- God's timing is not our timing when it comes to growth.
- We are called to be good stewards and let God grow the fruit.
- If we don't see growth, we can't give up but need to try again, maybe make changes, fertilize, do something different, or just wait because sometimes it's just a timing issue.
- Remember that God is in the middle of it all, for God is Creator of all and giver of life, not us.

The next step of linking with the agricultural-based narrative involved a narrative taken from a farming blog that talks about the frustrations in the *growing* season and the need to work in faith. Faithful and fruitful were the themes that resonated with all of the groups. When asked to reflect on the overarching message and the ways we are called to live faithfully in the *growing* season, one participant noted, "in the growing season you have to trust and have faith that God does His part; He is our rain and our sun and no matter how bad it looks, it's not as bad as it seems. Thank God, we don't need to have spiritual green thumbs to receive His blessings."

Session four brought the groups to the final season, the *harvest* season. Once again, I employed artwork of Vincent Van Gogh, this time his 1888 painting of "Harvest" and used Visio Divina for centering and prayer. From an agricultural perspective, the harvest season is defined as revolving around the product of the land and the work of the Lord to bring it to completion. Participants were asked to reflect on what they see, hear, and feel - physically, emotionally, and spiritually - in the harvest season.

Descriptors of the *harvest* season were as follows: smell of cut hay, reward for hard work, goodness of God, being ripe and ready, different colors, sharing of farm equipment and machinery, sharing with others, sense of community, busyness, a sense of completion, and ending. When talking about the local experience of the *harvest* season, one specific story from Prospect emerged that connected the community and the church, as a woman shared the following narrative:

> I remember the threshing machines going from house to house and it was often scheduled so it would be lunch time when they stopped at our house. That was the days when we were tenant farmers next door to the church. It was a time when farmers worked together. I remember we didn't get sodas that often but when it was harvest time, they had a milk cooler and would keep sodas in it. So, when all the work was finished, we could go get one. She added; You can still tell when its harvest season here at the church – it's hard to get in the front door for all the tomatoes and vegetables people have brought in. It was and still is a "take what you need' kind of offering.

In taking the descriptors of the *harvest* season and linking them with the story of the local church, participants were asked to share the time they saw said descriptors within their church's life story. Many noted times when work toward a specific project was completed, or a new ministry focus brought in new faces and needed dollars. Hard work, God's provision, and community effort were predominant themes, with a nod given to the inconvenience that was necessary to bring the work together.

Scriptures employed for the biblical link included Ruth 2:1-12 and Luke 12:13-21. From the Ruth passage, participants once again echoed the presence of community and provision as themes in the harvest season. A note was given about the roles of the different people mentioned in the Ruth passage and how it relates to the diverse community that is supposed to make up the church. Also noted was the concept that there was work for everyone to do. In the Luke passage, which was Jesus' parable about the farmer with bigger barns, the participants saw it as a caution in the harvest season. Participants gave similar responses that the farmer in the story had selfish motives and focused on trivial things in life. Many concluded that they cannot see the harvest in the church for what they get out of it but must see it as an investment in God's plan for unseen days ahead, all through the lens of "by His grace, and for His glory". Just as in parable, we need to be careful not to miss opportunities to yield more for the Kingdom.

With the *harvest* season in mind, the agricultural narrative for this section dealt with a farming community's response to a fatal farming accident and the need to bring in the crop. While the story shared happened in recent years, study participants began sharing stories they had experienced and heard over the years about farming accidents and how the farming community always came together to give emotional and physical support to the family or group in need. The discussion grew into the overarching theme of different jobs and different people for one purpose, much like the varied gifts for the One Body in One Spirit for One Lord.

The general consensus of all the groups was that God was in all parts of the harvest season, from the growth into fullness to the sharing of the fruit into the community.

One more session was offered as a concluding session for the study groups. In this session, the image given to ponder was a saying by Doe Zantamata: What you see depends on how you see the world; to most people, this is just dirt. To a farmer, it is potential. With the idea farming entails a plan and process; participants were encouraged to reflect on the idea that all seasons are cyclical in nature and thereby of equal importance to health and growth of the crops, as well as one's faith. The question was posed: how do we plan with "the end in mind" when it comes to being God's farm? This question then led to the question, "if we are God's farm for a purpose, what does scripture say about our purpose as followers of Christ"?

Scripture was once again used to help guide discussion, using Galatians 6;7-10; 2nd Corinthians 5:17, and Colossians 3:23. Echoes of the Great Commission and Great Commandment were heard across the group responses, along with reminders like: remember to be thankful and prayerful in all circumstances, we need to plant to reap what is sown, do good to all people, don't give up, don't be discouraged, don't grow weary, and you are the only Jesus some people will see.

Just as Ruth and Naomi remained faithful even when the landscape around them did not always seem promising, the new day was just ahead as we are all called to be faithful "in and out of season."

Chapter 5

N – NEED TO WORK THE LAND

Therefore, my dear friends, as you have always obeyed—not only in my presence, but now much more in my absence—continue to work out your salvation with fear and trembling.

(Philippians 2:12 NIV)

Missing one ingredient can make all the difference. Ask any of us who had Mom's famous pumpkin pie from Thanksgiving 1975. The pie was a golden orange with just enough browning on the crust and smelled delicious. We were all anxious to get our turn at having a piece of this holiday treat. Our forks at the ready, we dove in for that first bite, and all anticipation died in one fell swoop. My father, the diplomat in the group, said, "Beggy (that's what he called my mom), what recipe did you use?" Defenses rose as her tone of voice rose, "What do you mean? I used the same recipe I always did." And then, as all eyes were on her, she took a hefty bite, and her eyes widened. She put her fork down and said in a whisper, "I forgot the sugar." At that moment, my non-plussed father hugged Mom, went to the freezer, got out the vanilla ice cream, and saved the day. Years later, we would laugh about that pie but we remembered the message: check and double-check you haven't forgotten a step along the way.

Farming is a combination of good land stewardship and good investment of resources, incorporating all for the best results in the end. In flat terrain like southern Delaware, growers find the environment perfect for raising chickens in long chicken houses. With more chickens locally, more local grain is needed. Hay, soybeans and various vegetables benefit local farmers with additional goods for sale. Additionally, if one area of the field is prone to flooding, the farmer takes that into account when planting and planning for the harvest.

To reclaim our grounding of our true home, we can't leave out Christ or community. That's the reason the great commandment is to love God and love neighbor; without either, the main ingredient for a grounded faith would be missing. Unfortunately, food insecurity exists and is too easily overlooked. Economic inequity is seen in the workplace and in housing availability. Reaping justice alongside faith is a must to successfully grow our faith into a fruitful and abundant harvest that brings life to others. However, God's economy has to become the norm instead of the exception, an action we see come alive in the story of Ruth.

As Ruth Chapter 2 opens, a wealthy man named Boaz enters the story. Ruth volunteers to glean the harvest fields to pick up the stalks of grain left behind, as was the practice in the region. The grain left in the fields was intentional to help give dignity and opportunity to those in poverty who needed the food. Naomi told her to go ahead, and as God's providence would have it, Ruth found herself gleaning from a field who was a relative of her deceased father-in-law. As Boaz inquires about the industrious and hard-working Moabite woman gleaning his field, he is told how she looks out for her mother-in-law Naomi by picking up the food essential for their survival. An impressed Boaz wants to make sure she is not only successful in gathering the grain but also safe while she works. Ruth 2: 10-15 shows the scene in the field:

> At this, she bowed down with her face to the ground. She asked him, "Why have I found such favor in your eyes that you notice me—a foreigner?"

Boaz replied, "I've been told all about what you have done for your mother-in-law since the death of your husband—how you left your father and mother and your homeland and came to live with a people you did not know before. May the Lord repay you for what you have done. May you be richly rewarded by the Lord, the God of Israel, under whose wings you have come to take refuge."

"May I continue to find favor in your eyes, my lord," she said. "You have put me at ease by speaking kindly to your servant—though I do not have the standing of one of your servants."

At mealtime, Boaz said to her, "Come over here. Have some bread and dip it in the wine vinegar."

When she sat down with the harvesters, they offered her some roasted grain. She ate all she wanted and had some leftovers. As she got up to glean, Boaz gave orders to his men, "Let her gather among the sheaves and don't reprimand her. Even pull out some stalks for her from the bundles and leave them for her to pick up, and don't rebuke her."

Church is a community where spiritual farmers gather to grow together in a faith that brings good fruit for all. However, the 21st-century church is a consumer-driven church that must know the needs of its surrounding community to be relevant. Churches often "want" more people and more revenue, but "need" to be rooted in spiritual disciplines, so the growth comes from God.

Through listening and learning about the lay of the land about one's current physical location and then refining the listening and sharing process to assess and acknowledge the current situation, the time comes when hands need to get into the ground and work the land. And the work of the land may be similar to others but is unique to its grounded identity in Christ by its location, experiences, and spiritual health. Increased volume of fruit from the farm does no good if it lacks the goodness from being borne of healthy earth and plants.

However, change is not easy when the land has been turned upside down. Turning over soil is not just used to plant but also to pull up weeds from choke out new growth. However, as the parable tells us, sometimes one needs to let the weeds and the wheat grow together and let God do the sorting at the appropriate time.

Cultural change has deep roots, and the process of spiritual farming is an ongoing process over the years. The sharing of stories proved a way to open dialogue and possibilities, encouraging all to tend to the land in all seasons while encouraging the good that comes from diversifying our efforts across the life of our community.

Ruth brings a view of economically and socially marginalized people within our community, people, for various reasons, pushed to glean from the edges of the field. Ruth knew racism as being a Moabite was seen as not only with ethnic differences but also with religious differences. And yet, all blends into a story that speaks to not only learning but finding a grounded identity. An identity grounded not in location or societal differences, but in finding roots and shared traits of being made in the image of God. An image that reflects being wonderfully and fearfully made across time, across landscapes, and seasons.

As Ruth Chapter 2 comes to a close, Boaz's favor toward the young Moabite widow is seen by Naomi and begins to give her hope as seen in her statement, "you might be harassed in other fields, but you'll be safe with him" (ref. Ruth 3: 22). So ruth continued to work through the end of the barley harvest and then into the wheat harvest and "all the while she lived with her mother-in-law." During her season of changing landscape, work, and cultural shifts, Ruth stays faithful to the woman who has welcomed her into her home. For home is not as much a place as it is a state of heart and mind. The power of all of us being dirt-borne and shaped by the Creator reminds us of this truth when we lose our grounding.

The introduction and re-introduction of agrarian-based narratives planted new seeds and reconnected people to the biblical narrative and to the reality of where God has planted them in this life and on the land, they call home.

For with a change in season, diversity becomes the important fourth step to healthy growth on God's farm – in community and in self.

Chapter 6

D – DIVERSITY IN THE FIELDWORK

There is one body, but it has many parts. But all its many parts make up one body. It is the same with Christ. We were all baptized by one Holy Spirit. And so we are formed into one body. It didn't matter whether we were Jews or Gentiles, slaves or free people. We were all given the same Spirit to drink. So the body is not made up of just one part. It has many parts.

(1 Cor. 12:12-14 NIRV)

Just as a local dairy has multiple flavors of ice cream to draw people to its farm, people enter church through more than one door and for more than one reason. The farm and the small church must share the goal not just to survive but to thrive. Any farmer knows that diversification is necessary to survive in the 21st century. While the Gospel doesn't change, the small rural church's re-presenting of Christ to the community will make the difference in a living church or just an existing one. From the previous steps in the spiritual cultivation process for the small rural church, the strengths of the specific community of faith will be unearthed. Pairing congregational and community strengths with the power and perspective that God owns the church and God alone brings the growth creates fertile soil. The next steps in growing spiritual fruit are to have the courage to be different.

When I went to college, I attended a historically black university because it had the education program I was looking for, and it was within driving distance. Little did I realize the education I would receive would be more than a book alone could hold. In one of my first classes, over a hundred students filled the seats.

And every couple of weeks, the instructor would invite each student to come forward and check their current grade status. Like any inquisitive student, I went forward and waited in line for my turn. As his finger pointed to my grade, I noticed another notation written next to my name: white. Yes, I was one of three white students in a class filled with people of color. And until that time, I never thought about being singled out because of the color of my skin. Through my experiences at that university, and later during my years of seminary on a District of Columbia city campus, I would learn more about diversity firsthand than I had ever thought there was to learn. That inclusive community, as has been said, is not just being invited to show up, but also being asked to dance. And still, the soil of my soul has steadily needed cultivation, overturning again and again, for fresh growth of new fruits for God's Kingdom, which is rich with languages, ethnicities, and cultures.

However, not all attempts to bring diversity into familiar territory are met with welcome; as cultivation turns over ground, the process is often messy, stinky, and worms surface. But when worms can be seen aerating the ground, something new is ready to emerge.

To address the need for diversity in the landscape where one is located, three approaches prove helpful in discerning next steps: Mission, Action, and Prayer.

Diversity and ministry can be seen in engaging with mission opportunities at the local, regional, and global levels. Mission diversity should include a variety of encounters, not just sending a check. Personal interaction with a missionary or being able to be hands-on in the creation or presentation of items, or going on site, helps build relationships within diverse missional opportunities, increasing not only a gospel lesson for the receiver but also for the giver.

Diversity and action are essential to building relationships. Just as farming communities will often gather to support one another in times of need, like helping bring in the crops for a fellow farmer with cancer, cooperation and action come from coming alongside one another. Too often, if we keep an arm's length from those they are seeking to serve, an "us and them" dynamic can form, and opportunities for blessings can be missed. However, other areas need action to move simply from diversity being present to inclusion becoming part of the church's DNA. Relationships that include, and not just identify differences, can add layers of richness to our soul soil for growing Kingdom fruit.

One area of diversity moving into a more relationship-based inclusion can be seen in relationship building with people with disabilities. Historically, society has welcomed people with disabilities to taste and see that the Lord is good but has not included them to the level to which they were asked to take part in the preparation, planting, and harvesting of the land. With the passage of the Americans with Disabilities Act in 1990, the cry of "nothing for us without us" could be heard in the halls of the legislature and should be echoed in the halls of our churches. By expanding the diversity of local church action in mission from merely identifying people with needs to seeing the unique gifts, talents, and perspectives offered, gospel seeds can grow deeper roots.

Finally, diversity and prayer are the fertilizer for the crops we plan to grow for the Kingdom in our community. Personal prayer, corporate prayer, and focused prayer and fasting in certain seasons are all needed to not only discern next steps but to saturate the ground with trust in God, who is ever faithful. As the Apostle Paul writes, Creator God is the only One who can bring growth (ref. 1 Cor. 1 3:6-9 NCV)

It should be noted that change for change's sake does not necessarily transform, but diversifying our efforts to include more experiences that build relationships with the land and the people of the land, not only gives but to receives God's blessings. To be transformed by the diversity on God's Farm, ministry and mission must be included within our hearts and our lives, for that is where the transforming power of Christ brings new life. Looking beyond what we have always done to what we could do is what gives us vision, focus, and momentum to turn over new ground and begin planting new seeds.

Diversity is needed for our spiritual home base to be healthy as well. The Apostle Paul makes the case for diversity to the young churches struggling with their identity and grounding. A flowering tree can not bear fruit without being pollinated and connected to another living being, much different from itself. We can not bear fruit without allowing the "different" to teach us the fullness of God's creative glory. The Apostle Paul notes this in his letters to the churches (Romans 10:12, Galatians 3:28, Colossians 3:11) as the spiritual home where our faith is grounded has to be in the soil that gives life to all, not just those like me.

In Ruth Chapter 3, the scene opens on Naomi looking to help Ruth find her forever home with Boaz. But first, fieldwork of personal integrity and placement has to take place. After following her mother-in-law's direction, this young woman went where she was led, first to glean the field and then to seek a kinsman redeemer's favor from the threshing floor.

Usually, a woman who was a widow, and a foreigner at that, would be redeemed by her husband's nearest kinsmen, as it is written in Leviticus 25:25: *"If one of your fellow Israelites becomes poor and sells some of their property, their nearest relative is to come and redeem what they have sold."* Because of the law in the Torah,

Ruth went to the threshing floor and waited for Boaz to finish tending to the barley and then lay down for the night at Boaz's feet. This was a symbol of longing — to be redeemed by Boaz by society's standards. While the threshing floor is a physical space for chaff and edible rice to be separated, it symbolizes far more.

In the particular story of Ruth and Boaz, Ruth symbolizes the believer, while Boaz symbolizes the redeemer — which is the coming Lord Jesus Christ. From the field to the threshing floor to the town square, their journey continues until Ruth's situation is redeemed for good, as noted in Ruth 4:9-12.

> Then Boaz announced to the elders and all the people, "Today you are witnesses that I have bought from Naomi all the property of Elimelek, Kilion, and Mahlon. I have also acquired Ruth the Moabite, Mahlon's widow, as my wife, in order to maintain the name of the dead with his property, so that his name will not disappear from among his family or from his hometown. Today you are witnesses!"

> Then the elders and all the people at the gate said, "We are witnesses. May the Lord make the woman who is coming into your home like Rachel and Leah, who together built up the family of Israel. May you have standing in Ephrathah and be famous in Bethlehem. Through the offspring the Lord gives you by this young woman, may your family be like that of Perez, whom Tamar bore to Judah."

A new generation was created as Boaz was able to redeem Ruth and, in effect, the prophecy of Jesus happened. Ruth is one of the five women in Jesus' lineage who is named in the opening chapter of the Gospel of Matthew; the birthing a new hope occurred because the love of God and neighbor spanned over all seasons and all life fields within the hearts of those involved. Imagine what new possibilities could be borne if we too crossed political and social boundaries to honor the one who is Creator, Redeemer, and Savior of us all. What a diverse harvest awaits us when Kingdom equity reigns over the land of the new heaven and earth. Until then, let us keep open to the new and different God has in store for us all.

Chapter 7

LOOKING ACROSS THE HORIZON

See, I am doing a new thing! Now, it springs up; do you not perceive it?
I am making a way in the wilderness and streams in the wasteland.

(Isaiah 43:19 NIV)

Is Apollos important? No! Is Paul important? No! We are only servants
of God who helped you believe. Each one of us did the work God gave
us to do. I planted the seed, and Apollos watered it. But God is the One
who made it grow. We are God's workers, working together; you are
like God's farm..."

(1 Corinthians 3:5-6, 9 NCV)

Commencements happen all the time. Not just in the spring, when graduates celebrate the completion of a course of study. Not just in fall when the harvest is taken in from the fields. Not just when a child is born, a couple is married, or a loved one dies. Commencements are the ending of one thing, so the next can begin. And we all start somewhere.

The LAND process, outlined in chapters 2-5 with its spiritual grounding in our stories, cultivates spirituality amid cultural changes in order to bring hope and health to our community context. Like many processes, it is not easy, and it is a process that can be quickly finished. Seeking our identity through our spiritual home in the land where we live is an act of holiness that helps us find our way home to the Father.

Ecclesiastes 3:1 reminds us "to everything there is a season, and a time to every purpose under heaven": those words are true for the land of the farmer and of our faith, especially those whose faith sprouted in small rural churches. In 1925, a concern emerged for young people who were losing interest and leaving the farm; out of that concern, the Future Farmers of America (FFA) was born with 33 students in 18 states. Today, even with farming seen in a decline, all 50 states are currently chartered members with a mission to prepare future generations for the challenges of feeding a growing population.[53] At the 1978 FFA Convention, broadcast journalist Paul Harvey offered the address, "And God made a Farmer." Over the years, the National Farm Bureau began its Sunday convention session with the hymn, "Great is Thy Faithfulness," whose second verse was a reminder:

Summer and winter and springtime and harvest;

Sun, moon, and stars in their courses above,

Join with all nature in manifold witness

To thy great faithfulness, mercy, and love. [54]

And over the seasons, perspectives and centers of focus change. Currently, the National Farm Bureau no longer includes the God-praising hymn at the opening of the Sunday session at their annual convention. Yet, the FFA Creed of the agricultural based student organization still states the following hope within its creed: " I believe in the future of farming with a faith born not of words but deeds... the promise of better days through better ways, even as the better things we now enjoy come to us from the struggles of former years."[55] Likewise, the practices in our churches have changed, but our creedal foundation remains a true layer of the rich soil that brings life to our communities of faith.

Several decades have passed since broadcast journalist Paul Harvey offered words of encouragement to future farmers eager to show what they could do with the land. As long as people need to eat, farmers will be needed to work the land. And if there are folks living inside and outside of the city centers trying to find their way in the world, many will need to be spiritually fed with sustenance that only comes from the Creator of the Land. Tending the soil of our souls has to be found outside of ourselves. The Word of God, with its seeds of grace and truth, has stood the test of time and political powers and all of the challenges we face on this earth. If we are to find the landscape of our true home in eternity to come, we have to begin today, becoming the spiritual farmers of our soul soil as we help others in their journey of faith.

The challenge of a Christian is to be alive and not just exist, recognizing the demands of the current culture while ultimately standing on the truth that God's ways are not always humankind's ways. The challenge of spiritual farmers, believers who call this earth home for now, is to also not just attend church but to be the living witness of life in the Spirit.

So, in the style of Harvey's FFA address, I conclude with words of encouragement infused with God's Spirit to the Christians – the spiritual farmers - seeking to thrive in the 21st century in search of hope and health. It is not a word soaked in sentimentality, but the strength of relationship and life found on God's Farm:

> And on the 8th day, God looked down on his creation and said, "I need to pull a special group of people for a special mission in this world."
>
> – So, God raised you up to be a spiritual farmer
>
> God said, "I need some folks willing to meet out in the middle of nowhere with no phone signal found, a gathering place where they can talk about weather and politics and religion, and still work shoulder to shoulder to build me a house of prayer."

– So, God raised you up to be a spiritual farmer

"I need some folks who sing together, pray together, share, care, and dare together and sit down to a meal like family, and even if someone sits on their pew, they can still say 'I love you brother, I love you sister'. . . and mean it."

– So, God raised you up to be a spiritual farmer

God said, "I need some folks who are willing to let the worker come into the church without taking off his boots even though covered with mud, to let the farmer miss the trustee meeting because there are beans to get in before the rain, to let the sister sing off key and not kick her out of the choir because all can make a joyful noise, to let the babies cry and the toddlers whine during the service because it is a sign of life, and still have time to comfort the older confused member who can't remember the words any more but joins in with an "amen" at the end of each prayer"

– So, God raised you up to be a spiritual farmer

God had to have some people willing to travel in the cold and heat, and summer and winter, and day and night, by foot, by bike, by horse, or by whatever means necessary whenever the church doors are open just to worship the Almighty, All-knowing, All-powerful Creator God who has given them breath for that very day and very purpose

– So, God raised up spiritual farmers

God said, "I need some folks who believe I exist in places where two or three are gathered in my name, where the bank account is small but hearts are big, and where 'all lives matter' is not a political statement but a way of life.'"

It had to be a group of people who were willing to work hard for the Kingdom of God where they are planted – at the crossroads and in the fields and forests and on the sweeping plains across the land, equipped with and thankful for what they have, and who were willing to let God be God; a group of people who realize things of this earth are temporary but life in the Maker of Heaven and Earth is forever, and so they are willing to share, as the generations before them had done, the importance of faith and their messy but grace-filled role in growing fruit for God's farm – a group of people who have come to their senses and find that their roots, their home is not a place on the map or a person who is loved, but a Father who is infinite and intimate as the land we walk on.

So, God raised you up to be a spiritual farmer – on purpose for a purpose.

Thanks be to God.

APPENDIX I

Fieldwork Personal Study Guide: Six Sessions on Spiritual Seasons

---

Session 1: Seasons Change – Embracing God's Rhythms

Reading: Chapter 1 – *Seasons Change*

Season: Introduction to all seasons; foundational rhythms of land and soul.

Scripture:

- Ecclesiastes 3:1 – "To everything there is a season…"
- Genesis 8:22 – "As long as the earth endures… seedtime and harvest…"

Prayer Exercise:

Walk outdoors and observe the current season of the land. In prayer, ask: "God, what season am I in spiritually?" Listen in silence for several minutes. Journal your impressions.

Reflective Questions:

- Which season best describes your life right now—fallow, planting, growing, or harvest?
- How do you typically respond to change? How is God inviting you to respond?

Session 2: The Fallow Season – Trusting the Rest

Reading: Chapter 2 – *Preparing to Come Home*

Season: Fallow – a time of stillness, grief, and spiritual restoration.

Scripture:

- Exodus 23:11 – "Let the land lie fallow…"

- Psalm 23:2–3 – "He makes me lie down… He restores my soul."

Prayer Exercise:

Spend 10 minutes in silent prayer, inviting God to reveal where you need rest. End by slowly praying Psalm 23 aloud as a personal affirmation.

Reflective Questions:

- What in your life feels barren or paused?
- How might this fallow time be God's gift, not punishment?
- What are you grieving or letting go of in this season?

Session 3: Planting Season – Breaking Ground with Faith

Reading: Chapter 3 – *L: Listening and Learning from the Lay of the Land*

Season: Planting – the time of breaking ground, risk, and new beginnings.

Scripture:

- Hosea 10:12 – "Break up your fallow ground…"
- Matthew 13:3–9 – Parable of the Sower

Prayer Exercise:

Take a piece of paper and draw a seed. Inside the seed, write a dream or hope you're planting. Pray over it daily, asking God for courage to sow it with intention.

Reflective Questions:

- What new work or invitation from God is beginning in your life?
- What fears or resistances need to be broken up?
- How are you preparing the "soil" of your soul to receive?

Session 4: Growing Season – Nurturing What's Been Planted

Reading: Chapter 4 – *A: Assessment and Acknowledgement of the Ground*

Season: Growing – when roots deepen, identity forms, and perseverance is needed.

Scripture:

- 1 Corinthians 3:6–9 – "God gives the growth…"
- Luke 13:6–9 – The Barren Fig Tree

Prayer Exercise:

Draw or write a spiritual "growth chart" tracing a faith experience that took time to unfold. Name the challenges and the hidden work God was doing.

Reflective Questions:

- What habits or practices are sustaining your faith right now?
- What challenges are helping you grow?
- How has your identity in Christ deepened in this season?

Session 5: Harvest Season – Reaping and Rejoicing

Reading: Chapter 5 – *N: Need to Work the Land*

Season: Harvest – a time of fruitfulness, sharing, and legacy.

Scripture:

- Galatians 6:9–10 – "At the proper time we will reap a harvest…"
- Ruth 2:1–12 – Ruth gleans from Boaz's field

Prayer Exercise:

Make a gratitude list of the "fruit" you see in your life (relationships, growth, answered prayers). Offer a prayer of thanksgiving and ask: "How can I share this fruit?"

Reflective Questions:

- What are you harvesting in this season?
- How has your life or faith impacted others?
- What legacy of faith do you hope to leave?

Session 6: Living in the Land – Cultivating a Soil Culture

Reading: Chapter 6 & Chapter 7 – *D: Diversity in the Fieldwork* and *Looking Across the Horizon*

Season: All seasons – living rooted and responsive to God's ongoing work.

Scripture:

- 1 Corinthians 3:9 – "You are God's field…"
- Luke 15:20 – "While he was still a long way off…"

Prayer Exercise:

Find a quiet space and hold a handful of soil (or something symbolic). Pray: "Lord, make my heart good soil for Your kingdom work." Reflect on what God is planting in you now.

Reflective Questions:

- What does it mean for you to live rooted and ready?
- How is your spiritual community helping (or hindering) this?
- What next step is God calling you to take?

APPENDIX II

Fieldwork Small Group Study Guide:

Six Sessions on Spiritual Seasons and Our Stories

Session 1 – Seasons Change – Embracing God's Rhythms in the Land

Experience

In the movie, "Gone with the Wind" (1939), landowner and farmer Gerald O'Hara reminds his daughter Scarlett that she is an heir to the family plantation named Tara and that land is important to her identity and future. He says "Do you mean to tell me . . .that land doesn't mean anything to you? Why land is the only thing in the world worth workin' for, worth fightin' for, worth dyin' for, because it's the only thing that lasts".

- What is your experience with the word "heir"?
- Do you have something in your life you hope to pass down for generations to come?
- The word "land" brings varied images, feelings, experience. List words that describe your experience with land (e.g. what it looks like, what it feels like, what it reminds you of).
- O'Hara sees land as being important because "it's the only thing that lasts". This concept is one commonly found in farming communities. Why might this concept of "heir" and "land" be important to the church in the 21st century?

Explore

Land is important. God formed us of land. For that reason, we are connected to the land in a physical and spiritual way.

The LORD God took a handful of soil and made a man. God breathed life into the man, and the man started breathing. Genesis 2:7 CEV

From being formed in the Garden of Eden, to Noah's finding a place to land after the flood, to Abraham's leaving of his land of origin, to Joshua ushering a new era in the Promised Land, the role of land has always been key in the lives of God's people in the Old Testament. But it is more than just geography. Jesus, who was born in a farm structure, told 10 parables directly connecting the people to farming references.

Identity through connection is important. Author Ellen F. Davis in her book *Scripture, Culture, and Agriculture* noted this connection understood by those who stay close to the land. She writes:

> ". . . agrarians know the land, not as an inert object, but as a fellow creature that can justly expect something from us whose lives depend on it..." And YHWH God formed the human being ['adam], dust from the fertile soil ['adama]" Gen. 2:7). Although the wordplay is captured surprisingly well by the English pun "human from humus," the Hebrew is more fully descriptive of their family resemblance...
> it evokes the specific relationship between a people and their particular place".(pg.29)

As a farmer, the character Gerald O'Hara in the movie, knew that everyone needs a place of grounding that confirms their identity and their future. For Christians, and for the Church, that land is Christ.

Our role at God's Farm is important. Witness Lee once wrote in the *Purpose of God's Purpose by Christ's Fulfillment in us*, "A farm is a plot of land for growing things. The church is God's land to grow Christ, not in an individual way, but in a corporate way. . . something of Christ will be grown up in each of us". (p.54).

As Paul writes in 1 Corinthians 3:9, "you are God's cultivated field [His garden, His vineyard] . . . We are God's farm, and it is from the land that we can gain not only identity, but also direction on how to bear fruit for the Lord.

Engage

As followers of Christ, we can find our way through the spiritual geography of our individual lives and of the life of our church as we reclaim the importance of the land in our lives.

- Share a story about a time when you needed to get away and you went to "the land" to find your grounding. Explain: what prompted you to go, where you went, and what was the result of your "getting away to the land"?
- Share the story of how your church came to be on the location where it currently exists. Why would location be important for a community of faith to be grounded?

In the Bible, locations such as Hebron, Bethel, Mt. Horeb, and the River Jordan all have a significance in the identity of a people by their experience of God in that place.

- What specific place or location holds spiritual significance for you and why?

Extend

Diana Butler Bass writes *in Grounded: Finding God in the World – A Spiritual Revolution:*

God is the ground, the grounding, that which grounds us. We experience this when we understand that soil is holy, water gives life, the sky opens the imagination, our roots matter, home is a divine place, and our lives are linked with our neighbors' and with those around the globe. This world, not heaven, is the sacred stage of our times. (pg. 26)

In our lives and our churches, we go through seasons similar to the seasons of the land. The seasons are as follows:

The Fallow Season – when the climate and the land are not conducive to widespread planting in the natural outdoors. As such, planting and growing are at a standstill; this may look like the winter season of empty fields.

The Planting Season – when the climate and the land are ready to be prepared to receive seed and new plantings; this may look like the spring season with overturned soil and seeds going into the ground.

The Growing Season – When the climate and the land have received the seed and the growing process is underway; this may look like the summer season when growth comes from the seed and matures into the desired crop.

The Harvest Season – when the growing is completed, and the finished crop is taken out of the field to be dispersed in various ways; this may look like the fall season when crops are brought in and the harvest celebrated.

In looking at the seasons above, which season best represents the current season of your life? The current season of your church's life?

Gleanings from Lesson One

During the week, it is helpful to go back and review the lesson. It is not required, but sometimes sitting with scripture and stories can help us grow spiritually. If there are any questions you didn't answer during the session, now may be a time to sit with the question to seek the answer that comes to you.

You are encouraged to journal, writing down your thoughts or stories that come to mind, or to write prayers specific to the season you just discussed. Either way, spend some time re-visiting this season as a personal reflection for yourself and your church.

Day One - What words currently describe my spiritual life?

Day Two - If I could imagine a landscape that reflects your spiritual life, what would it look like? Describe it.

Day Three - What words currently describe my church's spiritual life?

Day Four - Imagine a physical landscape that reflects your church's spiritual life. What would it look like? Describe it.

Day Five - What words or prayer would you like to say to God about the current spiritual condition around yourself? What questions do you have? What praises do you have?

Session 2: The Fallow Season

Experience

From an agrarian perspective, the fallow season is when fields are bare and nothing seems to be growing. For many, this season is experienced as the season known as winter. In looking out over the fields in the winter or fallow season, what do you see and hear? What do you feel – physically, emotionally, and spiritually?

Explore the Everyday Story

One church felt the fallow season in this way:

My church has been experiencing a fallow season for probably 10-15 years, due to decline in the number of people attending worship services, Sunday school, Bible study, and youth group. I grieve for the time when all of these activities were full of people. We say, "I remember when . . ." We say, "Someone needs to step up and do . . ." and, "The younger people should be taking on the responsibilities". We all have different opinions on what is wrong or why nothing much seems to be growing, or why younger families do not participate in the life of the church.

We have talked some about what we should do to grow our church attendance, focusing on what we think should happen and without focusing on what God would have us do. We do not, usually, make or carry out plans. We do not often talk about how we can reach out to others in love, in Jesus' name. I don't think we all love whoever walks through our doors. And that goes for the newcomers and some who have been here a while. It feels like there is a lot of lack of communication, conflict over situations and lack of a spirit of love among members". Those empty spaces in the pews feel cold and lonely, hard – even with their cushioning. There are times this season seems long and unending.

- How does this story echo the descriptive words you used under your "experience" of the fallow season?
- Share an example of how your church felt during a fallow season.

Engage the Biblical Story

Read the following passages and reflect on who is involved, what is going on and why?

Exodus 23:11-12

Jeremiah 32:1-25.

Habakkuk 3:17-19

How are the characteristics we listed for the fallow season seen in these passages?

Story Linking Process.

Take the descriptions given in the Experience section and compare with reflections on the everyday story. Then compare and link with the biblical story. Use guiding questions below.

What similarities and feelings resonate with the biblical story and the everyday story?

Where is God in the fallow season as seen in the everyday story and the biblical narratives?

Extend the Agricultural Narrative

Read the following and discuss this excerpt from Julie Peter's Spirituality and Health blog, "the Fallow Field: The Virtue of Doing Nothing" https://spiritualityhealth.com/blogs/downward-blog-a-life-in-yoga/2014/03/06/jc-peters-fallow-field-virtue-doing-nothing.

We live in a world that privileges work, productivity, and speed, so when I take the time to do nothing in particular, I feel guilty. I am not carpe-ing any diems here. So why do I feel such a strong need to sit on my couch and watch TV shows from the early nineties?

I think it's for the same reason growing fields need to sometimes lie fallow. Farmers will occasionally plough a field that normally grows a crop like corn or wheat, and simply not seed it for that growing season. The blank, unseeded space is a "fallow field."

During this time of apparently nothing, the soil is regenerating, and restoring its fertility so that by next season it will be ready to grow. The farmers don't treat the soil, inject it with fertilizers, plant better seeds, or poke at it with a magic wand. They just get out of the way.

We are a culture of human doings, not human beings. We are not in the habit of taking time off to let the body and mind do their mysterious internal work . . . It's hard to trust that just because you can't see growth or changes doesn't mean it isn't happening.

Giving my instincts a chance to talk to me passively can be helpful. Sometimes it's also a little scary: if I give myself the space to think and feel properly, I might discover that I need to change something . . . Trust your fallow field, and it will be ready when the growing season comes.

Highlight the parts of this story that connect to descriptors of the Fallow Season and to other parts of the everyday story and biblical story. Then,use the story linking process to continue to make connections between all four sections. *If time to explore the questions below, do so in small groups. If no time remains, encourage participants to explore these questions, write down their thoughts, and bring them to the next session.*

- What message seems to emerge for your individual life and for the life of a congregation?
- What is a way God calls us to live faithfully in the Fallow Season?

Gleanings from Lesson Two

During the week, it is helpful to go back and review the lesson. It is not required but sometimes sitting with scripture and stories can help us grow spiritually. If there are any questions you didn't answer during the session, now may be a time to sit with the question to seek the answer that comes to you.

You are encouraged to journal, writing down your thoughts or stories that come to mind, or to write prayers specific to the season you just discussed. Either way, spend some time re-visiting this season as a personal reflection for yourself and your church.

Day One – What was the most important thing I learned about myself and the fallow season?

Day Two – What was the most important thing I learned about my church and the fallow season?

Day Three – What do I see as the greatest challenge of the fallow season?

Day Four – What do I see as the greatest opportunity in the fallow season?

Day Five – What words or prayer would you like to say to God about the fallow season? What questions do you have? What praises do you have?

Session 3: The Planting Season

Experience

From an agricultural perspective, the planting season is when ground is turned over to make room for a new planting and plans are put into motion to fertilize and nurture the new growth emerging. In the planting season, a farmer must often cultivate – pull up and turn over – the soil by reshaping it so it can accept the seed and water needed to grow. Imagine looking out over the fields in the planting season, what do you see and hear? What do you feel – physically, emotionally, and spiritually?

Explore the Everyday Story

One church felt the planting season in this way:

The planting season at our church was when we decided to put new life in our congregation. We began planting seeds by having sermons and studies about what it meant to be a disciple because I think some of us had been doing it (church) so long, we had forgotten . . . We started looking for ways to plant seeds outside of the church, beginning with collecting change for missions and then looking for events happening in town that we could be a part of. That took getting over some attitudes and preconceptions we had – but it was breaking new ground, a kind of turning over ground so we could plant more seeds. . . You can't plant seeds if you stay within the walls of the church . . . you can do the planning and preparing there, but you also have to go outside.

How does this story echo the descriptive words you used under your "experience" of the planting season? Share an example of how your church felt during a planting season.

Engage the Biblical Story

Read Mark 4:3-9, 13-20. Who is in the story, and what is going on?

Read John 12:24. How are the characteristics we listed for the planting season seen in these passages?

Story Linking Process.

Take the descriptions given in the Experience section and compare them with reflections on the everyday story. Then compare and link with the biblical story. Use the guiding questions below

What similarities and feelings resonate with the biblical story and the everyday story?

Where is God in the planting season as seen in the everyday story and the biblical narratives?

Extend the Agricultural Narrative

Read the following in pairs, then discuss this excerpt from Noah Sanders' book, *Born Again Dirt*:

One of my older Christian neighbors was once approached by an extension agent who asked, "Mr. Hay, I have noticed that every year you have a beautiful garden. What is your secret?" My neighbor replied in his deep, dignified southern accent, "Well, first we work hard to prepare the soil for planting. Then we look in the almanac to see what day would be good for planting according to the moon, for the Bible says the moon was created to mark the times and seasons. And after we get everything in the ground, I go sit on the log over by the side of the garden, take off my hat, and pray, "Lord, we've done the best we know how. Now it is up to you to give us a good garden". I don't think that extension agent went around telling Mr. Hay's secret to a good garden, but I think

Mr. Hay hit the nail on the head. Our job is to be faithful and the fruit is up to the Lord.

Many of us farmers struggle with worry. When there are so many things out of our control, we tend to worry about whether all our hard work will pay off in the end. However, Christ commands us not to worry. He provides for the birds and the flowers, and He will provide for us if we are faithful and obedient to Him. When the Lord does bless us, we need to acknowledge that the increase of the land is a gift of God, not an automatic right that we have because of our work. May we never boast save in the Lord" (pp.17-18).

Highlight the parts of this story that connect to descriptors of the Planting Season and other parts of the everyday story and biblical story. Then, use the story linking process to continue to make connections between all four sections. *If time to explore the questions below, do so in small groups. If no time remains, encourage participants to explore these questions, write down their thoughts, and bring them to the next session.*

What message seems to emerge for your individual life and the life of your congregation? What is a way God calls us to live faithfully in the Planting Season?

Gleanings from Lesson Three

During the week, it is helpful to go back and review the lesson. It is not required, but sometimes sitting with scripture and stories can help us grow spiritually. If there are any questions you didn't answer during the session, now may be a time to sit with the question to seek the answer that comes to you.

On the space below, you are encouraged to journal, writing down your thoughts or stories that come to mind, or to write prayers specific to the season you just discussed. Either way, spend some time re-visiting this season as a personal reflection for yourself and your church.

Day One – What was the most important thing I learned about myself and the planting season?

Day Two – What was the most important thing I learned about my church and the planting season?

Day Three – What do I see as the greatest challenge of the planting season?

Day Four – What do I see as the greatest opportunity in the planting season?

Day Five – What words or prayer would you like to say to God about the planting season? What questions do you have? What praises do you have?

Session 4: The Growing Season

Experience

From an agricultural perspective, the growing season is defined as a time when conditions are favorable for growth; a time when fruit begins to emerge, a time when challenges are encountered but perseverance prevails. In looking out over the fields in the growing season, what do you see and hear? What do you feel – physically, emotionally, and spiritually?

Explore the Everyday Story

One church felt the growing season in this way:

We went through a growing season within our church when we started to grow in size. We had to adjust the "this is the way we always did it attitude" to a group of people who were coming and had never done church that way. It meant making allowances for children who were not always quiet in service. It meant we needed to put step stools in the restrooms so children could reach the sink; we never had those before. It meant making a ramp so the one person with a walker would have an easier time getting in the building; and don't you know it – then other folks brought friends who had walkers and made use of the ramp. Many of us old timers had to get in the habit of saying our name; instead of thinking everyone already knew it. And we found we started to grow closer as our family grew. Not everyone was happy about the growth and some disagreements crept in. Some folks left. Most folks stayed. In all of it, we tried to keep the main thing the main thing. . . that was, we were called to be faithful disciples – love God and love others, even others we didn't know - and God would take care of the growth.

How does this story echo the descriptive words you used under your "experience" of the growing season? Share an example of how your church felt during a growing season.

Engage the Biblical Story

Read Matthew 13:24-20, Matthew 13:31-32 and Luke 13:6-9. Who is in each passage and what is going on? Then read 1 Corinthians 3:6-9. How are the characteristics we listed for the growing season seen in these passages?

Story Linking Process.

Take the descriptions given in the Experience section and compare with reflections on the everyday story. Then compare and link with the biblical story. Use guiding questions below.

What similarities and feelings resonate with the biblical story and the everyday story?

Where is God in the growing season as seen in the everyday story and the biblical narratives?

Extend the Agricultural Narrative

Read the following excerpt from Christine Hoover's blog entitled, *Three Lessons from the Farmer about Faith* (http://www.desiringgod.org/articles/three-lessons-from-the-farmer-about-faith.)

Farming is backbreaking work, dirty work, detailed work, and, most of all, it is risky work. There aren't any guarantees. A few years ago, Travis reminded me, when the crop stood beautiful and bountiful in the fields, ready for harvest, a hurricane blew through the Rio Grande Valley and wiped it away entirely. All that labor, all that grime, all that waiting, for nothing.

What is the point? Why would we invest everything in a risky venture? We might ask this, thinking of our own lives and our own efforts to produce a spiritual harvest and have seemingly harvested nothing or been wiped out entirely.

The farmer looks at his failed crop as a tangible reminder that the harvest inevitably belongs to the Lord. The farmer must be faithful to lay the groundwork for the harvest, but the harvest cannot be forced; it can only happen through the Lord's providence.

There are things that pop up in the growing season that aren't helpful or what you want to see. We get rain that we don't want on the crops. I've learned not to go look at the crops on the day it rains, because that's when it looks the worst. It's never as bad as we thought after we come through it, though, and even what doesn't look good is working toward the end goal of the harvest. In the end, no matter what the crop looks like, we have to trust God that he's going to take care of us. To focus on fruitfulness is a frustrating endeavor; to work in faith is all we are asked to do. And it's really all we can do.

Highlight the parts of this story that connect to descriptors of the Growing Season and to other parts of the everyday story and biblical story. Then, use the story linking process to continue to make connections between all four sections. *If time to explore the questions below, do so in small groups. If no time remains, encourage participants to explore these questions, write down their thoughts, and bring them to the next session.*

What message seems to emerge for your individual life and for the life of your congregation? What is a way God calls us to live faithfully in the Growing Season?

Gleanings from Lesson Four

During the week, it is helpful to go back and review the lesson. It is not required but sometimes sitting with scripture and stories can help us grow spiritually. If there are any questions you didn't answer during the session, now may be a time to sit with the question to seek the answer that comes to you.

On the space below, you are encouraged to journal, writing down your thoughts or stories that come to mind, or to write prayers specific to the season you just discussed. Either way, spend some time re-visiting this season as a personal reflection for yourself and your church.

Day One – What was the most important thing I learned about myself and the growing season?

Day Two – What was the most important thing I learned about my church and the growing season?

Day Three – What do I see as the greatest challenge of the growing season?

Day Four – What do I see as the greatest opportunity in the growing season?

Day Five – What words or prayer would you like to say to God about the growing season? What questions do you have? What praises do you have?

Session 5: The Harvest Season

Experience

From an agricultural perspective, the harvest season is defined as a time when the product and the work have come to a completion. Imagine looking out over the fields in the harvest season, what do you see and hear? What do you feel – physically, emotionally, and spiritually?

Explore the Everyday Story

One church felt the harvest season in this way:

> It had taken three years of planning, preparing, tearing down, building up, and raising funds for it all to come together, but it finally did. Our Capital Improvement Campaign was complete. We had begun with a prayer asking God to provide and we ended giving God the glory for His provision. Our restoration and renovation project began with just a trickle of donations, but then more and more hands helped out. Some pulled out old flooring and plumbing. Others put new carpet and bathroom fixtures. All were inconvenienced at some point, but it was worth it in the end. It wasn't easy, but together we collected over $200,000 without incurring debt and enlisted hundreds of man hours. The new improvements helped us financially give more to mission and be more effective in our mission and ministry as the church. And it was all God. We can't boast about it because God did what we couldn't. All the praise goes to God.

How does this story echo the descriptive words you used under your "experience" of the harvest season? Share an example of how your church felt during a harvest season.

Engage the Biblical Story

Read Ruth 2:1-12 and Luke 12:13-2. Who is in each passage and what is going on? Then re-visit 1 Corinthians 3:6-9. How are the characteristics we listed for the harvest season seen in these passages?

Story Linking Process.

Take the descriptions given in the Experience section and compare with reflections on the everyday story. Then compare and link with the biblical story. Use guiding questions below.

What similarities and feelings resonate with the biblical story and the everyday story?

Where is God in the harvest season as seen in the everyday story and the biblical narratives?

Extend the Agricultural Narrative

Read the following in pairs then discuss this news story broadcast by WBOC News in Salisbury Md. (http://www.wboc.com/story/32420785/farming-community-rallies-behind-killed-parsonsburg-man).

LAUREL, Del. - The farming community in western Sussex County came together Sunday afternoon, just two days after a Parsonsburg, Md. farmer lost his life on a Laurel, Del. farm. It was on Friday that 61-year-old Michael Griffin was working on a "Bale Bandit", when he got caught, pulled inside, and killed.

"He was definitely a gentleman farmer", said Robert Smith, a close friend. "He's the kind of person where there aren't many of them left. He would give you the shirt off his back, if you needed a hand. He was there."

Griffin died while working on Smith's field. Griffin's death left more than just aching hearts. He also left a lot of work to do, since he ran a flourishing business baling more than 500 acres per year across Sussex County. With his death, Griffin's family would have lost a lot of income, and so the farming community decided to chip in.

"We decided we were going to do it for them", said Jessica Smith. "And then everybody from every direction wanted to bale. They wanted to help. They wanted to do this."

All in all, Smith said more than 100 people volunteered to help bale the Smith property, and in the end, they completed approximately 50 acres.

"All farmers came together for one farmer yesterday", Jessica said. "It's great. None of us are family, but when you farm, everyone's a family. It's you know one person is in need and it's kind of like a big family. They're all willing to help."

"He would just have a big smile on his face", said Robert. "One-hundred-percent. I can see him right now just looking down just smiling."

Highlight the parts of this story that connect to descriptors of the Harvest Season and to other parts of the everyday story and biblical story. Then, use the story linking process to continue to make connections between all four sections. *If time to explore the questions below, do so in small groups. If no time remains, encourage participants to explore these questions, write down their thoughts, and bring them to the next session.*

What message seems to emerge for your individual life and for the life of your congregation? What is a way God calls us to live faithfully in the Harvest Season?

Gleanings from Lesson Five

During the week, it is helpful to go back and review the lesson. It is not required but sometimes sitting with scripture and stories can help us grow spiritually. If there are any questions you didn't answer during the session, now may be a time to sit with the question to seek the answer that comes to you.

You are encouraged to journal, writing down your thoughts or stories that come to mind, or to write prayers specific to the season you just discussed. Either way, spend some time re-visiting this season as a personal reflection for yourself and your church.

Day One – What was the most important thing I learned about myself and the harvest season?

Day Two – What was the most important thing I learned about my church and the harvest season?

Day Three – What do I see as the greatest challenge of the harvest season?

Day Four – What do I see as the greatest opportunity in the harvest season?

Day Five – What words or prayer would you like to say to God about the harvest season? What questions do you have? What praises do you have?

Session 6: Living in the Land – Cultivating a Soil Culture

Experience

Stephen Covey, author of "The 7 Habits of Highly Effective People", listed Habit Two as "Begin with the End in Mind." Farmers have employed this habit long before Covey's 1989 book. The harvest that one seeks has to be in one's mind before buying seed, tilling the ground, or even planning for the care of the growing plant. When undertaking an endeavor, there must be a plan – even if it gets changed along the way – to reach a desired result.

> Questions to consider: What do you think about the quote by Doe Zantamata that "what you see depends on how you see the world: to most people this is just dirt; to a farmer, it is potential." What kind of seeds do we "plant" in our lives? What end result do we hope for? At our church, how do we plan with "the end in mind" when it comes to being God's farm?

Explore

We are God's farm for a purpose – to yield a harvest for the Kingdom. According to author Peter Walker in his book, *The Bible and the Land: An Encounter,* he writes, "In the Christological logic of Paul the Land (like the law), particular and provision have become irrelevant" The land for him has been "christified." It is not the Promised Land that became his "inheritance" but the Living Lord, in whom was a new creation. . ." Walker continues that "to be "in Christ". . . has replaced being in the land as the ideal life...for the promised land signifies the Kingdom of God. (112-114) "

How do the following scriptures inform us and our churches to be God's farm for a purpose? Galatians 6:7-10; 2 Corinthians 5:17; Colossians 3:23-24. What do you see as the purpose for your church? What are you called to do with the "land" God has given you?

Engage

In Kathleen Norris' book, *Dakota: A Spiritual Geography,* she tells of Hope Presbyterian church as located by itself in the South Dakota Prairie. The church is the neighborhood church that understands the power of community and working together for the good of God. Norris describes it in the following way:

> *Hope's members take seriously their responsibility as members of the world's diverse and largely poor human race. . . in recent hard times, while Hope's membership declined by nearly half, the amount the church donates for mission has increased every year. It now ranks near the top in per capita giving among Presbyterian churches in the state of South Dakota.*

> *Hope is where I realized how much the members of a rural church actually work as well as worship together. They live supporting each other. . . it's a power derived from smallness and lack of power, a concept the apostle Paul would appreciate. . .*

> *He (one pastor) said, "City people want hymns that reassure them that God is at work in the world, but the people in the western Dakotas take that for granted. (pp.166-168). "*

Small and rural churches are as important as the small farms that are scattered across our county. While these churches may seem insignificant to the 21st century culture around us, God assures us we are called according to God's purpose and plan. We are told in Zechariah 4:10a. *"Do not despise these small beginnings, for the LORD rejoices to see the work begin..." NLT.* How do you hear hope for your life and your congregation in Norris' experience?

Extend

Ellen F. Davis writes the following in "Scripture, Culture, and Agriculture,"

> *"A contemporary prayer delineates accurately the biblical understanding that our intended service to the land is a holy obligation precisely because it is part of our service to God: Give us all a reverence for the earth as your own creation, that we may use its resources rightly in the service of others and to your honor and glory..."(30)*

Throughout this study we have looked at our connection to the land and what it looks like to live in the four spiritual seasons. Seasons are cyclical; all seasons come and go in a cycle. We also experience seasonal cycles in the life of our church based on the church year, based on the calendar year, and based spiritually on our growth as God's farm. We are never meant to stay stuck in one season but to continuously be growing and dying to self so we can grow even more. We must remember that the harvest for us is not about building kingdoms or stockpiles for ourselves but building the Kingdom of God now and to come.

With that in mind, discuss and answer the following questions:

What season are you currently experiencing in your life? Is it different from the beginning of this study? What season is your congregation currently experiencing? Is it the same or different than what you thought at the beginning of this study? What message has God given you on how to live faithfully in this season? Within your current season, how can you connect with your community and share the Good News? What questions do you still have about being faithful as God's farm?

Gleanings from Lesson Six

During the week, it is helpful to go back and review the lesson. It is not required, but sometimes sitting with a scripture and stories can help us grow spiritually.

> Sit quietly for one minute with one thought, "We are God's church." After that time, what images come into your mind? What words, scriptures, or songs come to mind? What does God want you to know about being God's farm?

> Take at least 5 minutes to sit with these thoughts, then offer a prayer to God, thanking Him for His faithfulness and provision in each season.

ENDNOTES

Chapter One

[1] Witness Lee, "Fulfillment of God's Purpose by the Growth of Christ in Us. (Anaheim, CA: Living Stream Ministry Publishing, 1965) 54.

[2] James Weldon Johnson, "The Creation", God's Trombones: Severn Negro Sermons in Verse, (New York: Penguin Books, 2008) 17.

[3] Dietrich Bonhoeffer, Creation and Fall (Minneapolis, MN: Fortress Press, 2007) 76.

[4] Bonhoeffer, Creation and Fall, 77.

[5] Ellen Davis, Scripture, Culture and Agriculture: An Agrarian Reading of the Bible (New York: Cambridge University Press, 2009) 29.

[6] Walter Bruggeman, The Land: Place as Gift, Promise, and Challenge in Biblical Faith (Minneapolis, MN: Fortress Press, 2002) xiii.

[7] Bruggeman, The Land, 62.

[8] Bruggeman, The Land, 168.

[9] Lisa Loden, Peter Walker, and Michael Wood, ed., The Bible and the Land: An Encounter: Different Views: Christian Arab Palestinian, Israeli Messianic Jew, Western Christian (Jerusalem: Musalaha, 2000) 133-134.

[10] Hymn of Promise, Accessed 12/30/2016, http://hymntime.com/tch/htm/h/y/m/hymnprom.htm

[11] T.S. Eliot, "East Coker" from The Four Quartets poems, Accessed 2/2/2018, http://oedipa.tripod.com/eliot-2.html

[12] Natalie Sleeth, Hymn of Promise", The United Methodist Hymnal (Nashville, TN: The United Methodist Publishing House, 1989) 707.

[13] Thurman, Howard, Deep is the Hunger (New York: Harper and Row, 1951) 89-90.

[14] M. Craig Barnes. Searching for Home: Spirituality for Restless Souls. (Grand Rapids, MI, BrazosPress, 2003). 17.

[15] Frederick Norwood, The Story of American Methodism. (Nashville, TN: Abingdon Press, 1974) 159-160.

[16] Aaron Earls. "Small Churches Continue Growing – In Number, Not Size." Accessed 3/21/2025, https://https://research.lifeway.com/2021/10/20/small-churches-continue-growing but-in-number-not-size/

[17] Walter Bruggeman. The Land: Place as Gift, Promise, and Challenge in Biblical Faith. (Minneapolis, MN: Fortress Press. 2002.) xxii.

[18] Bruggeman, The Land, 1.

[19] Bruggeman. The Land, 4.

[20] Bruggeman. The Land, 5.

[21] Bruggeman. The Land, 173.

[22] Kathleen Norris. Dakota: A Spiritual Geography, (New York: First Mariner Books, 2001.) 37.

[23] Norris, Dakota, 167-168.

[24] Norris, Dakota, 164.

[25] Norris, Dakota, 164.

[26] Bruggeman, The Land, 15-16.

[27] Jurgen Moltmann. God in Creation (Minneapolis, MN: Fortress Press, 1993) 51.

[28] Moltmann, God in Creation, 186.

[29] Diana Butler Bass, Grounded: Finding God in the World – A Spiritual Revolution (New York: HarperOne, 2015) 26.

[30] Butler Bass, Grounded, 58.

[31] Butler Bass, Grounded, 58.

[32] Davis, Scripture, Culture and Agriculture ,38.

[33] Ernest Kurtz and Katherine Ketcham, The Spirituality of Imperfection: Storytelling and the Search for Meaning (New York: Bantam Books, 1992) 42.

[34] Kurtz, The Spirituality of Imperfection, 19.

[35] Howard Thurman, Disciplines of the Spirit. (Richmond, IN: Friends United Press, 1963) 21.

[36] Daniel J. Stulac, "A Gospel of the Ground", Plough Quarterly (Walden, NY: Plough Publishing House, Spring 2015) 28.

[37] Stulac, "A Gospel of the Ground", 27.

[38] Bailey, The Holy Earth, 26.

[39] Masanobu Fukuoka, The One-Straw Revolution (New York: New York Review Book, 1978) 21.

[40] Fukuoka, The One-Straw Revolution,113.

[41] Golemon, Larry A. Ed., Finding Our Story: Narrative Leadership and Congregational Change (New York: The Alban Institute, 2010) 11.

[42] Goleman, Finding Our Story, 17.

[43] Mann, Alice, "Place-Based Narratives: An entry point for ministry to the soul of a community," Finding Our Story: Narrative Leadership and Congregational Change (New York: The Alban Institute, 2010) 59.

[44] Mann, Finding Our Story, 74-75.

[45] Tom Berlin and Lovett H. Weems, Jr. High Yield: Seven Disciplines of the Fruitful Leader. (Nashville, TN: Abingdon Press. 2014) 19

[46] Sanders, Noah, Born-Again Dirt: Farming to the Glory of God, (Rora Valley Publishing, 2012) 17-18.

[47] Masanobu Fukuoka, The One Straw Revolution, Rodale Press,1978, xiv.

[48] Wendell Berry, The Unsettling of America: Culture and Agriculture (Counterpoint, 1977).

Chapter Three

[49] Howard Thurman, Deep is the Hunger (Friends United Press, 1951) 48.

[50] Thruman, Deep is the Hunger, 49.

[51] Anne E. Streaty Wimberly, Soul Stories: African American Christian Education, (Nashville, TN: Abingdon Press, 2005), 26.

[52] Sensing, Qualitative Research, 158.

[53] FFA History, Accessed May 21, 2018, https://www.ffa.org/about/what-is-ffa/ffa-history

Chapter Seven

[54] "Great is Thy Faithfulness", The United Methodist Hymnal (Nashville, TN: The United Methodist Publishing House, 1989) 140.

[55] FFA Creed, Accessed May 21, 2018, https://www.ffa.org/creed

BIBLIOGRAPHY

Adeyemo, Tokunboh. *Africa Bible Commentary*, Grand Rapids. Zondervan. 2006.

Bailey, L.H.. The Holy Earth. Michigan State University Press. 2008.24, 26

Bartlett, David and Barbara Brown Taylor, ed. *Feasting on the Word, Year A, Vol. 1*. Louisville. Westminster John Knox Press, 2010.

Bass, Diana Butler. *Grounded: Finding God in the World – A Spiritual Revolution*. New York. HarperOne, 2015.

Berlin, Tom and Lovett H. Weems, Jr. *High Yield: Seven Disciplines of the Fruitful Leader*. Nashville: Abingdon Press. 2014.

Berry, Wendell. "Standing By Words". Berkley: Counterpoint, 2008.

Berry, Wendell. *The Mad Farmer Poems*. Berkeley: Counterpoint, 2013.

Berry, Wendell, *The Unsettling of America: Culture and Agriculture*. Counterpoint, 1977.

Bonheoffer, Dietrich. *Creation and Fall*. Minneapolis: Fortress Press, 2007.

Bruggeman, Walter. *The Land: Place as Gift, Promise, and Challenge in Biblical Faith*. Minneapolis: Fortress Press. 2002.

"Church Health Survey Results Analysis Packet for Wesley United Methodist Church, Georgetown, DE from the Lawless Group". Received by Wesley UMC Church Council, October, 2016.

"Commentary on 1 Corinthians 3:1-9".
https://www.workingpreacher.org/preaching.aspx?commentary
_id=1950. Accessed 6/19/2016.

Covey, Steven. *The 7 Habits of Highly Effective People*. New York: Simon and Shuster, 1989.

Davis, Ellen. *Scripture, Culture and Agriculture: An Agrarian Reading of the Bible*. New York: Cambridge University Press, 2009.

"Delaware Agricultural Statistics".
www.nass.usda.gov/Statistics_by_State/Delaware. Accessed May 1, 2018.

The Discipleship Study Bible, NRSV, Louisville: Westminster John Knox Press, 2008

Eliot, T.S.. "East Coker" from The Four Quartets poems.
http://oedipa.tripod.com/eliot-2.html, Accessed 2/2/2018.

Future Farmers of America. http://www.ffa.org/about/whatt-is-ffa/ffa-history. Accessed May 21, 2018.

Fukuoka, Masanobu. *The One-Straw Revolution*. New York: New York Review Books. 1978.

Golemon, Larry A., ed. *Finding Our Story: Narrative Leadership and Congregational Change*. New York: The Alban Institute, 2010.

Hahn, Heather. "Places of the heart: Rural church at crossroads".
http://www.umc.org/news-and-media/places-of-the-heart-rural-church-at-crossroads, Accessed 10/9/2017.

Hamilton-Poore, Sam. *Earth Gospel*. Nashville: Upper Room Books, 2008.

Hauerwas, Stanley and L. Gregory Jones, ed. *Why narrative? Readings in narrative theology.*

Eugene, Oregon: Wipf and Stock Publisher, 1997.

"Inheritance", Bakers Evangelical Dictionary of Bible Theology. http://www.biblestudytools.com/ dictionaries/bakers-evangelical-dictionary/.html, Accessed 6/20/2016.

Johnson, James Weldon. "The Creation". *God's Trombones: Seven Negro Sermons in Verse.*

New York: Penguin Books, 2008.

Kurtz, Ernest and Katherine Ketcham. *The Spirituality of Imperfection: Storytelling and the Search for Meaning.* New York: Bantam Books, 1992.

Lacroix, Len and Jennifer Lacriox. "The Beauty of Brokenness", *Seeking the Lord* (blog), http://len-seekingthelord. logspot.com/2011/07/beauty-of-brokenness.html. Accessed 6/5/2016

Lee, Witness. *"Fulfillment of God's Purpose by the Growth of Christ in Us.* Anaheim, CA: Living Stream Ministry Publishing, 1965.

Lisa Loden, Peter Walker, and Michael Wood. ed., *The Bible and the Land: An Encounter: Different Views: Christian Arab Palestinian, Israeli Messianic Jew, Western Christian.* Jerusalem: Musalaha, 2000.

Mann, Alice. "Place-Based Narratives: An entry point for ministry to the soul of a community". *Finding Our Story: Narrative Leadership and Congregational Change.* Herndon, VA: The Alban Institute, 2010.

Moltmann, Jurgen. *God in Creation.* Minneapolis, MN: Fortress Press, 1993.

Morgan, Elisa. *The Orchard: A parable.* Grand Rapids, MI: Revell, 2006.

Moschella, Mary Clark. "Enlivening Local Stories through Pastoral Ethnography." *Teaching Our Story: Narrative Leadership and Congregational Change*. Herndon, VA: The Alban Institute, 2010.

Nee, Watchman. *The Release of the Spirit*. New York: Christian Fellowship Publishers, 2014.

Norris, Kathleen. "*Dakota: A Spiritual Geography*". New York: First Mariner Books, 2001.

Norwood, Frederick. *The Story of American Methodism*. Nashville, TN: Abingdon Press, 1974.

Nouwen, Henri. *Spiritual Formation: Following the Movements of the Spirit*. New York: HarperOne, 2010.

"Number of local churches as distributed by average attendance at the principle weekly worship service and by annual conference". http://www.gcfa.org/data-services-statistics. Accessed 10/2/17

Pappas, Anthony G. *Entering the World of the Small Church*. Herndon, VA: Alban Institute, 2000.

Parks, Lewis A. *Preaching in the Small Membership Church*. Nashville: Abingdon Press. 2009.

Parks, Lewis A. *Small on Purpose: Life in a Significant Church*. Nashville Abingdon Press, 2017.

Peters, Janet. "The Fallow Field: the Virtue of Doing Nothing". *Science and Health* (blog). https://spiritualityhealth.com/blogs/downward-blog-a-life-in-yoga/2014/03/06/jc-peters-fallow-field-virtue-doing-nothing. Accessed 1/2/2017.

Raloff, Janet. "Dirt is not Soil." https://www.sciencenews.org/blog/science-public/dirt-not-soil, Accessed 10/26/2018.

Sa, Kyung-Hee. "Dover District Churches Journal Statistics from 2012, 2013, 2014. Peninsula Delaware Conference of The United Methodist Church". Report presented at Dover   District clergy meeting January 2016.

Robinson, Robert H. and Daniel G. Coston Jr. *Old Country Churches of Sussex County, DE*. Georgetown, DE: Sussex Prints. 1976.

"Rural Life Sunday". https://www.umcdiscipleship.org/resources/rural-life-sunday. Accessed 4/1/2018.

Sanders, Noah. *Born-Again Dirt: Farming to the Glory of God*. Rora Valley Publishing. 2012.

Lyle E. Schaller. *Small Congregation, Big Potential: Ministry in the Small Membership Church*. Nashville: Abingdon Press, 2003.

Tim Sensing, *Qualitative Research: A Multi-methods Approach to Projects for Doctor of Ministry Theses*. Eugene, OR: Wipf and Stock, 2011.

Sheldrake, Philip. *Spirituality: A Brief History*. West Sussex, UK: Wiley-Blackwell. 2013.

Stulac, Daniel J. "A Gospel of the Ground". *Plough Quarterly*. Walden, NY: Plough Publishing House. Spring 2015.

The United Methodist Hymnal. Nashville, TN: The United Methodist Publishing House, 1989

Thomas, Robert B. *The Old Farmer's Almanac 2018*. Dublin, NH: Yankee Publishing   Incorporated, 2017.

Thurman, Howard. *Deep is the Hunger.* New York: Harper and Row. 1951.48, 49

Howard Thurman, *Disciplines of the Spirit* (Richmond, IN: Friends United Press, 1963) 21.

"Times and Seasons of the Agricultural Year." https://www.churchofengland.org/ prayer-and worship/worship-texts-and-resources/common-worship/churches-year/ times-and-seasons/agricultural-year Accessed 4/1/2018.

U. S. Department of Agriculture Economic Research Services Rural Classification. http://www.ers.usda.gov/topics/rural-economy-population/rural-classifications/what is rural.aspx . Accessed 5/15/2018

Vang, Preben. *Teach the Text Commentary Series: 1 Corinthians.* Grand Rapids, MI. Baker Books. 2014.

Williams, William H. *A History of Wesley U.M. Church: Georgetown 1779-1978.* Georgetown, DE: The Countian Press. 1978.

Wimberly, Anne E. Streaty. *Soul Stories: African American Christian Education.* Nashville: Abingdon Press. 2005.

ABOUT THE AUTHOR

Rev. Rebecca "Becky" Kelly Collison, an ordained Methodist pastor, holds a bachelor's degree in special education from University of Maryland Eastern Shore, a master's in education from Wilmington (College) University, and a Master of Divinity and Doctor of Ministry, both from Wesley Theological Seminary in Washington, DC. When not at the parsonage of her current pastoral appointment, she lives with her husband, Glenn, on the corner of the family farm in Harrington, Delaware, and enjoys the company of family, including their six children and seven grandchildren.